THE
NATIONAL
PARKS

THE NATIONAL PARKS

A VISUAL HISTORY OF ALL 58 NATIONAL PARKS

MEL WHITE

Quercus

CONTENTS

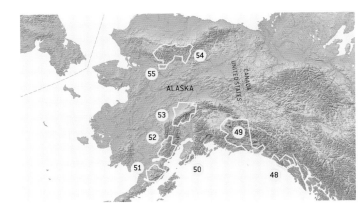

NATIONAL PARKS OF THE UNITED STATES

ROCKY SEACOASTS, TROPICAL CORAL REEFS, vast deserts, active volcanoes, alpine tundra, near endless cave passageways, awe-inspiring forests, expansive icefields—the diversity encompassed within the national parks of the United States is unsurpassed by the protected areas of any other country. America's 58 national parks preserve an outstanding sampling of natural environments, home to thousands of species of animals and plants, from whales and giant sequoias to hummingbirds and orchids.

The circles on this map show a concentration of parks in the western mountains and the Colorado Plateau. At the time that America's system of national parks was coming into existence, in the late 19th and early 20th centuries, largely unpopulated tracts of public land were abundant in these regions. It was a relatively simple task to designate protected sites in spectacular (but often inhospitable) areas that became parks such as Crater Lake, in Oregon, Rocky Mountain, in Colorado, and Glacier, in Montana. By then the opportunities for creating parks in the densely settled East were limited. The last major frontier for national parks came in Alaska, with the designation of parks such as Wrangell-St. Elias and Gates of the Arctic in 1980. The most recently created national parks were the result of changes in status of existing areas, such as Cuyahoga Valley (from national recreation area in 2000) and Congaree (from national monument in 2003).

Old or new, accessible or remote, all the national parks of the United States reward a visit, combining scenery, wildlife, recreation, and history in ways that entertain and educate the casual visitor, the serious explorer, and everyone in between.

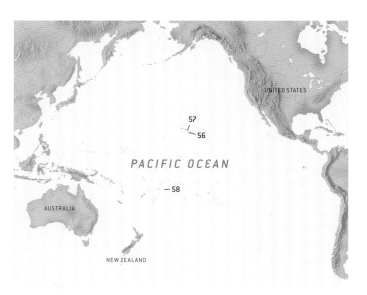

1 ACADIA NATIONAL PARK	8 BISCAYNE NATIONAL PARK	15 BADLANDS NATIONAL PARK	22 GREAT SAND DUNES NATIONAL PARK AND PRESERVE
2 CUYAHOGA VALLEY NATIONAL PARK	9 DRY TORTUGAS NATIONAL PARK	16 WIND CAVE NATIONAL PARK	23 MESA VERDE NATIONAL PARK
3 SHENANDOAH NATIONAL PARK	10 VIRGIN ISLANDS NATIONAL PARK	17 GLACIER NATIONAL PARK	24 CARLSBAD CAVERNS NATIONAL PARK
4 GREAT SMOKY MOUNTAINS NATIONAL PARK	11 HOT SPRINGS NATIONAL PARK	18 YELLOWSTONE NATIONAL PARK	25 GUADALUPE MOUNTAINS NATIONAL PARK
5 MAMMOTH CAVE NATIONAL PARK	12 ISLE ROYALE NATIONAL PARK	19 GRAND TETON NATIONAL PARK	26 BIG BEND NATIONAL PARK
6 CONGAREE NATIONAL PARK	13 VOYAGEURS NATIONAL PARK	20 ROCKY MOUNTAIN NATIONAL PARK	27 ARCHES NATIONAL PARK
7 EVERGLADES NATIONAL PARK	14 THEODORE ROOSEVELT NATIONAL PARK	21 BLACK CANYON OF THE GUNNISON NATIONAL PARK	

ATLANTIC OCEAN

UNITED STATES

CUBA

JAMAICA

HAITI

DOMINICAN REPUBLIC

PUERTO RICO

INTRODUCTION

OF ALL THE HUNDREDS OF PROTECTED areas within the United States and its territories, 58 have been awarded the designation of national park: sites especially distinguished by the beauty of their scenery, the majesty of their natural features, the pristine state of their ecosystems, the significance of their history, or the abundance and diversity of their flora and fauna. These national parks represent the best of natural America, and many of them rank with the most important wild places on Earth.

In *National Parks*, readers will find spectacular large-format photographs of all 58 national parks, as well as information on each park's outstanding features, from geological formations to wildlife to recreational opportunities. Maps locate major roads and key attractions, and visitor information for each park includes telephone numbers and websites. Parks are arranged generally east to west, beginning with Acadia National Park in Maine and continuing through the continental United States, Alaska, and Hawaii, and ending with the National Park of American Samoa in the southern Pacific Ocean.

A virtual voyage through this book will reveal the breathtaking beauty and vast diversity of America's national parks, opening doors to understanding more about these treasures and perhaps inspiring travel—both to celebrated parks and to those that are lesser-known and farther afield.

The United States national park system created a model for other countries in the protection of natural resources, but in its early years it was a disorganized effort, as America struggled to find ways to save and manage the best parts of its varied landscape. Awe-inspiring geysers and other geothermal features led to the establishment on March 1, 1872, of Yellowstone National Park—America's, and the world's, first national park. Although management responsibility was given to the federal Department of the Interior, for years Yellowstone suffered from lack of funding. Souvenir hunters vandalized rock formations, poachers slaughtered wildlife, and tourist facilities popped up without oversight. In 1886, U.S. Army Cavalry units arrived to police the park, although this would be only a temporary solution.

New names were added to the list of America's national parks: Sequoia and Yosemite in 1890, Mount Rainier in 1899, Crater Lake in 1902. In 1903, Wind Cave became the first national park in the world to protect a cave; in 1906, Mesa Verde became the first national park created to protect human-built archeological features, rather than natural resources. In the meantime, America was also designating national military parks and national monuments. Some were administered by the Department of the Interior, others by the United States Forest Service or the Department of War.

In 1916, President Woodrow Wilson signed legislation creating the National Park Service, charged with administering parks and monuments "to conserve the scenery and the natural and historic objects and the wild life therein and to provide for the enjoyment of the same in such manner and by such means as will leave them unimpaired for the enjoyment of future generations." Over time, the National Park Service became the managing agency not only for national parks and monuments but for battlefields, historic sites, rivers, seashores, trails, motor parkways, and other protected areas.

Today, the National Park Service operates with a budget of more than $2.5 billion, administering 84 million acres of land (55 million of that area in Alaska) in nearly 400 units, ranging in size from 13.2-million-acre Wrangell-St. Elias National Park and Preserve in Alaska to Thaddeus Kosciuszko National Memorial in downtown Philadelphia, Pennsylvania, just 0.02 acres in extent. Encompassed within the National Park Service are more than 5,000 historic buildings, more than 700 campgrounds, more than 8,000 monuments and statues, more than 13,000 miles of trails, and more than 2,400 miles of scenic rivers.

While all units within the National Park Service reward visits, the gems among America's protected areas are those 58 areas given the status of national parks, defined in part as "generally large natural places having a wide variety of attributes, at times including significant historic assets." Some, such as Grand Canyon National Park, are known around the world and receive millions of visitors annually. Others, such as Kobuk Valley National Park—located in a roadless area of Alaska above the Arctic Circle—may see fewer than 1,000 visitors in a year.

The earliest national parks were created in the vast forests, mountains, and badlands of the American West—a relatively simple process of designating protected areas in virtually unpopulated regions. It was not until 1919 that a national park was established in the more settled lands east of the Mississippi River: Lafayette National Park in Maine, now called Acadia. In 1926, Great Smoky Mountains, Shenandoah, and Mammoth Cave joined the list of eastern national parks, to be followed by superb sites such as Isle Royale, in Lake Superior, and Everglades in Florida.

The acreage administered by the National Park Service increased significantly in 1980 with the passage of the Alaska National Interest Lands Conservation Act, a controversial measure that created or increased the size of 15 national parks, preserves, and monuments. Thanks in part to this legislation, more than 85,000 square miles of America's largest state are permanently protected from most types of development. Some of the National Park Service lands in Alaska and elsewhere are designated as national preserves rather than national parks—a compromise between conservationists and pro-development forces that allows some hunting, trapping, and mineral extraction in lands that otherwise would qualify for national park status because of their outstanding natural value.

To explore fully the range of biodiversity and geological features encompassed within America's national parks would be the work of several lifetimes. Crocodiles cruise the subtropical waterways of Everglades National Park, while Gila monsters crawl through the desert of Arizona's Saguaro National Park, and muskoxen face the long, bitter winters of Gates of the Arctic National Park and Preserve in Alaska. Some of the most varied and colorful creatures within the national parks are found under water, around the coral reefs of Virgin Islands National Park and the National Park of American Samoa. Great Smoky Mountains National Park in the Appalachians ranks among the world centers for the small

Giant sequoia trees tower overhead in Sequoia National Park, in the Sierra Nevadas of eastern California. The world's largest trees in terms of volume, giant sequoias can reach more than 300 feet in height. Sequoia National Park is administered in conjunction with Kings Canyon National Park, to the north. Designated wilderness encompasses more than 720,000 acres of the two parks.

amphibians called salamanders, while Big Bend National Park, on the Rio Grande in a remote part of western Texas, is known as one of the country's most popular destinations for birdwatchers.

The terrain within Everglades National Park varies only a few feet in elevation; by contrast, Death Valley National Park features the lowest site in North America (282 feet below sea level) and an 11,049-foot mountain summit just 12 miles away. Denali National Park in Alaska contains the highest point in North America, 20,320-foot Mount McKinley, while California's Sequoia National Park boasts the tallest peak in the lower 48 states, 14,505-foot Mount Whitney (not to mention the giant sequoia trees that are arguably the Earth's largest living things).

Volcanic eruptions have been continuing for more than a quarter-century at Hawaii Volcanoes National Park. At Mount Rainier National Park in Washington, geologists keep a close eye on the park's centerpiece, an active volcano that

stands ominously near heavily populated urban areas. Yellowstone, of course, is America's most famous geothermal site, containing two-thirds of the world's geysers, evidence of tremendously violent volcanic eruptions in the far-distant past.

Guidebooks and websites can help a traveler prepare for a visit to a national park, but one often overlooked piece of advice is simply this: Take time to talk with rangers. Sometimes a few simple questions—"What's a good trail for a family with children?" or "How long does it take to hike to Chasm Lake?"—can make the difference between a pleasant visit and one that is memorable for the wrong reasons. When a park ranger says to carry a gallon of water on a long day hike in the desert, it is not because he or she wants to burden you unnecessarily: It is because without that water your trek could be miserable, or even deadly.

In many parks, statistics reveal the somewhat dismaying fact that the majority of visitors never venture more than a

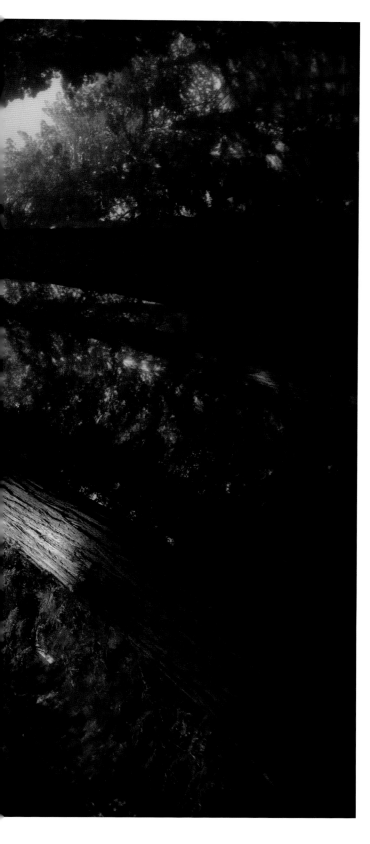

One of the most distinctive geological features of Utah's Arches National Park, Delicate Arch has been called "the most famous arch in the world." Eroded from reddish sandstone, it is among more than 2,000 arches in the National Park. Erosion continues its relentless work here, causing some arches to fall while continually sculpting new rock formations.

hundred feet or so from roads or other developed areas. While much can be seen from highways—Trail Ridge Road, in Colorado's Rocky Mountain National Park, is one of the most spectacular drives in the world—to experience a park at its best requires time spent exploring forests, meadows, deserts, rivers, lakes, and mountains on a more intimate scale. Nearly every national park offers a selection of short, easy interpretive nature trails suitable for all visitors, as well as long-distance hikes into remote wilderness. Rangers lead regular nature walks and campfire programs that can add new levels of enjoyment and appreciation to a park visit.

With adventure comes responsibility, though. Each year national park rangers conduct hundreds of rescue operations, most of which could have been avoided with foresight and preparation on the part of visitors. Adequate clothing (especially sturdy footwear and outer layers to add in case of bad weather), plenty of water, a good map, a flashlight, and an awareness of your own abilities and the difficulties of prospective routes—all these would prevent

many perilous situations and injuries. The solitude that adds so much to a backcountry hike can be dangerous if the help that is needed is far away. The point, then, is to do everything possible to avoid needing help.

National parks face continuing challenges in many arenas. Regional development has starved Everglades National Park of the water it needs for the health of its wetlands ecosystem. The glaciers of Glacier National Park may disappear by the year 2030 in the face of global climate change. Pollution degrades underground streams in Mammoth Cave. Political pressures can adversely affect management of some parks, such as allowing snowmobile use in Yellowstone. Yet polls show Americans strongly support national parks, and such backing provides perhaps the best hope that solutions can be found for problematic issues.

Many people have been influential in the development of America's national parks. The works of artist Thomas Moran helped bring attention to Yellowstone. Legendary

wilderness advocate John Muir worked to promote Yosemite and Sequoia National Parks. Businessman-philanthropist John D. Rockefeller Jr. played a part in protecting parks such as Acadia, Virgin Islands, and Grand Teton. Conservationist Marjory Stoneman Douglas brought public attention to the Everglades. Presidents such as Theodore Roosevelt and Jimmy Carter left important legacies of protecting the country's natural resources. Thousands of others, not so well known, have worked to create, expand, or defend national parks, many of them by serving as volunteers in parks.

As a result, millions of visitors from all over the world are able to experience the splendor and variety of America's national parks, from a quiet canoe trip on a wilderness lake to a strenuous mountain ascent to a dawn stroll down a forest path to enjoy bird song.

All those who have visited national parks surely hope that they will endure "for the enjoyment of future generations" with their beauty and diversity intact.

ACADIA NATIONAL PARK

NATURE MELDS REWARDINGLY WITH civilization at Acadia National Park, where wild, rugged seacoast lies just minutes from small-town shops and inns, where parkland intermingles with private property, and where mountaintop views take in uninhabited islands as well as a busy harbor. This juxtaposition results from the park's unique history, as a national park was created in an area that was already a popular tourism destination.

Most of the park lies on Mount Desert Island, located just off the coast of Maine and connected to the mainland by a bridge. Two sections of the park are disjunct from the island: an area of the Schoodic Peninsula to the east, and another tract on Isle au Haut, a small island to the south. All three parts of the park feature lush forests and spectacular scenery, including the wave-battered rocky coast for which Maine is famous.

Mount Desert Island was named in the early 17th century by the French explorer Samuel Champlain, the French word *"desert"* indicating a treeless, barren place. (Champlain was describing the rocky tops of the hills, not the island as a whole.) By the late 19th century, the beauty and peaceful character of the island had made it a summer retreat for some of America's wealthiest families—names such as Vanderbilt, Astor, and Ford—who built mansions along the coast near the town of Bar Harbor.

In the early 20th century, some residents became concerned by development of Mount Desert, eventually leading to the acquisition of land for what was first a national monument, elevated to national park status in 1919—the first national park established east of the Mississippi River. Acadia's boundaries today constitute a patchwork on the island, with national park land occupying much of the southeastern part of Mount Desert, while much of the western and northern sections are private property. Another of the wealthy part-time residents had a major influence on the park. John D. Rockefeller Jr. created a system of carriage roads winding 45 miles through Acadia.

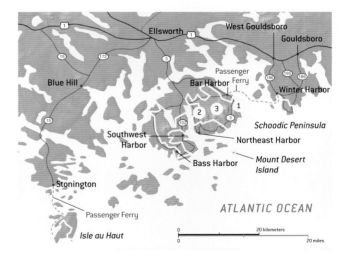

ACADIA SOUTHEASTERN MAINE

AREA
47,750 acres (193 sq km)
ESTABLISHED
February 1919
VISITOR INFORMATION
(207) 288 3338;
www.nps.gov/acad

KEY ATTRACTIONS ① Park Loop Road ② carriage roads ③ view from Cadillac Mountain
NOTABLE WILDLIFE White-tailed deer, porcupine, beaver, harbor seal, peregrine falcon, common eider, boreal chickadee

A classic example of a "drowned coast" inundated by rising sea level, the rocky shoreline of Acadia receives the force of waves crashing in from the Atlantic Ocean, resulting in a landscape of cobblestone beaches and dramatically eroded boulders. The Park Loop Road offers splendid views of the coast's granite cliffs and ledges.

Wide enough for horse-drawn carriages but closed to motor vehicles, these roads today offer a wonderful way to explore the park on foot, by bicycle, or on horseback. Seventeen stone-faced bridges make up part of the carriage-road system, each of a unique design for its particular location. In winter, the roads provide routes for cross-country skiing and snowshoeing.

The most popular single activity within Acadia National Park is undoubtedly traveling the 27-mile Park Loop Road, which passes through forest to skirt the island's coast, providing access to sites such as Thunder Hole (waves entering a hole in the rocks create a sound like thunder), the beautiful Otter Cliffs area, and Jordan Pond, a scenic glacier-sculpted lake in the middle of the island.

A 3.5-mile side route from the Park Loop Road leads to the top of Cadillac Mountain, the tallest mountain along the Atlantic coast of the United States. At 1,530 feet, Cadillac's summit at certain times of the year is the first place in the country to be touched by the Sun's dawn rays. Watching the sunrise here is a Mount Desert tradition. A short nature trail leads around the pinkish granite that makes up

the peak, while the splendid view encompasses Bar Harbor, Frenchman Bay, and the rounded shapes of the Porcupine Islands.

Hikers can enjoy 125 miles of trails crisscrossing the park, ranging from easy strolls to steep, strenuous routes up mountainsides. Red squirrels chatter anxiously at passers-by, while snowshoe hares freeze beside the path, hoping not to be seen. White-tailed deer bound away, tail "flags" flying, and a lucky hiker might spot a moose feeding in a wetland, though this large member of the deer family is rare on the island. Parts of some trails are closed seasonally to protect nesting peregrine falcons.

Glaciers scraped across what is now Mount Desert Island in several ice ages, retreating only about 15,000 years ago. The landscape that visitors see today—U-shaped valleys holding ponds in their basins, glacial erratics (boulders carried by glaciers and deposited by melting ice), and sheer cliffs—is in large part the work of ice. Mount Desert's most famous glacial feature is Somes Sound, the narrow bay that almost splits the island in two. The sound is the only true fjord on the eastern coast of the United States.

Built in 1858, the Bass Harbor Head lighthouse rises from a rocky headland at the southwestern tip of Mount Desert Island. The 32-foot-tall brick structure, one of the enduring symbols of Acadia, still helps ships find their way into Bass Harbor, using a Fresnel lens installed in 1902.

Tidepools along the park's coast hold an amazing array of colorful life, from barnacles and limpets to starfish and crabs. Park rangers lead seasonal field trips to explore tidepools, and this can be a good way to learn about the fascinating world at the interface of land and sea. Ship Harbor is a fine place for tidepooling, in the southwestern part of Acadia. Nearby Bass Harbor Head Lighthouse, though not publicly accessible, is one of the iconic symbols of Mount Desert and can be viewed from adjacent trails.

Located on the mainland about a half-hour drive from Mount Desert, the park's Schoodic Peninsula offers more stretches of rocky coastline, as well as excellent views back toward Mount Desert. A 6-mile drive loops to the tip of the peninsula, providing access to hiking trails and a short side road to the top of Schoodic Head, 440 feet above the sea and a great viewpoint. Other worthwhile trips near Mount Desert include a visit to remote Isle au Haut, accessible only by mail boat and offering 18 miles of little-travelled hiking trails; and ranger-led boat cruises to Baker Island and Little Cranberry Island.

Forty-five miles of gravel carriage roads wind through Acadia, the legacy of work done by businessman and philanthropist John D. Rockefeller Jr. in the 1930s. Closed to motor vehicles, these paths feature 17 historic stone-faced bridges, each designed to complement its location.

CUYAHOGA VALLEY NATIONAL PARK

ONE OF THE COUNTRY'S NEWEST national parks, Cuyahoga Valley was designated a national park in 2000, having been created as a national recreation area in 1974. In its suburban setting (between the Ohio cities of Cleveland and Akron), in its mixture of public and private lands, and in its history, it occupies a unique place in the national park system. Its existence is testimony, as well, to environmental restoration efforts and the dedication of local conservationists.

The name Cuyahoga comes from a Native American (possibly Algonquin) term meaning "crooked river." Early in the 1800s, a canal was built parallel to the Cuyahoga River to transport goods between Lake Erie and the Ohio River. The region became a focal point of recreation as far back as the 19th century, when residents drove carriages or took boat rides in the valley.

Local interest in creating a park grew in the 20th century, despite the Cuyahoga's extremely polluted condition, a consequence of industrial and residential wastes flowing into the waterway. Coincident with the creation of a National Recreation Area, clean-up efforts began that helped restore wildlife to the Cuyahoga River. Today, dozens of species of fish swim in the river, and waterside areas are home to wildlife including bald eagles, great blue herons, white-tailed deer, beaver, mink, and muskrats.

Much of the park is composed of eastern hardwood forest, with areas of conifers including pine, spruce, and hemlock. Meadows, old fields, and wetlands contribute to the diversity of flora and fauna. The central attractions of the park are a 22-mile section of the Cuyahoga River and the Towpath Trail, where hikers and bikers follow the route once used by mules pulling barges on the Ohio and Erie Canal. Eleven trailheads within the park provide access to the trail, which also extends beyond the park, both north to Cleveland and south to Akron. In all there are more than 125 miles of hiking trails in the national park, from the much trodden main routes to isolated paths perfect for birdwatching and other quiet forms of nature study.

Among the park's 70 waterfalls is Brandywine Falls, where a creek cascades down a series of picturesque waterfalls in a sandstone gorge. At Tinkers Creek Gorge is Bridal Veil Falls,

Great blue herons, long-legged wading birds that feed on fish, frogs, and other wetland prey, have returned to the Cuyahoga River Valley to breed and are now seen commonly in the national park. Once heavily polluted, the river has been the focus of intensive clean-up efforts that have once again made it a haven for wildlife.

where a frothing sheet of water is created along the creekbed. Another striking natural attraction is the Ledges, in the southeastern region of the park, where a trail system loops through hemlock forest around a plateau providing expansive views of the surrounding area.

A scenic train, the Cuyahoga Valley Scenic Railroad, operated by a nonprofit volunteer group, passes through the park. Besides regular sightseeing trips, the train provides a way for hikers and bikers to make one-way trips on the Towpath Trail, returning via train to their trailhead. Other popular draws include four golf courses, two ski resorts, and lodging facilities (none operated by the National Park Service). The Hale Farm and Village is a living-history museum with costumed interpreters providing a look at typical 19th-century pioneer farm life in Ohio. The Blossom Music Center, also within the park boundary, is the summer home of the renowned Cleveland Orchestra and offers other musical events throughout the season.

The park has several visitor centers, including the Canal Visitor Center, where an operating lock demonstrates how boats ascended and descended on the canal; the Boston Store Visitor Center, located in a restored 1836 general store; and the Peninsula Depot Visitor Center in the community of Peninsula.

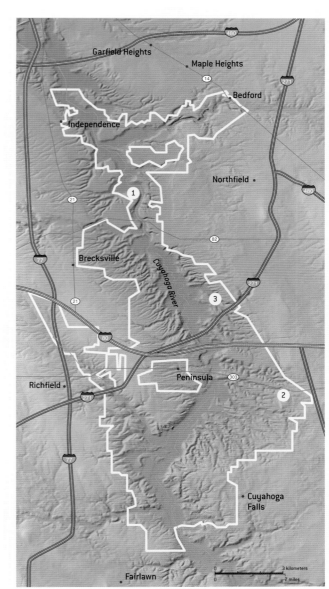

CUYAHOGA VALLEY NORTHEASTERN OHIO

AREA
18,440 acres (75 sq km)
ESTABLISHED
October 2000
VISITOR INFORMATION
(216) 524 1497;
www.nps.gov/cuva

KEY ATTRACTIONS ① Towpath Trail ② The Ledges ③ Brandywine Falls
NOTABLE WILDLIFE White-tailed deer, beaver, mink, bald eagle, great blue heron

SHENANDOAH NATIONAL PARK

VIEWS OF FORESTED RIDGES AND VALLEYS stretching to the horizon give only a hint of the wonders within this long and relatively narrow park in western Virginia. Protecting a portion of the Blue Ridge Mountains, the easternmost range of the Appalachian Mountains, Shenandoah National Park combines beauty, diverse flora, and an intriguing human history to reward a range of travelers, from wilderness backpackers to visitors on a casual scenic drive.

The Shenandoah River Valley to the west gave the park its name; to the east stretch the foothills of Virginia's Piedmont region, between the Appalachians and the Atlantic Coastal Plain. The Blue Ridge range makes up the park's major landscape feature, a terrain of steep-sided mountains, compact valleys, rocky streams, and waterfalls. The process of photosynthesis carried on by millions of trees results in water vapor being given off into the atmosphere. This slightly bluish natural haze persisting over the highlands was the origin of the name "Blue Ridge."

Running through the park like a spine from north to south, 105-mile-long Skyline Drive follows the crest of the Blue Ridge range. Reached by any of four entrances, the famed route is highlighted by 75 overlooks, which taken together offer a breathtaking album of some of the most beautiful scenery in the eastern United States. All the park's major attractions can be reached from Skyline Drive, and all are easily located thanks to the mileposts located along the way, numbered beginning at zero at the northern end. At its southern terminus, Skyline Drive connects with the Blue Ridge Parkway, a National Park Service-administered scenic drive that winds southward 469 miles to Great Smoky Mountains National Park.

Many park visitors see only the views from Skyline Drive, never getting more than a short distance from the roadway. There is far more of Shenandoah to enjoy, though, beginning with more than 500 miles of trails. Running approximately parallel to Skyline Drive, the Appalachian National Scenic Trail passes through the park for 101 miles on its way from Georgia to Maine. Although this path—probably the most famous hiking trail in America—is favored by long-distance backpackers, day-hikers can access it from many points along Skyline Drive for short walks.

Whether looking out from a drive viewpoint or along a remote trail, visitors from late May to June enjoy the park's blooming azaleas and mountain laurel, a colorful spectacle that ranks near the top of Shenandoah's delights. The delicate dark-pink azalea blossoms and the rounded clusters of light-pink mountain laurel flowers can in places make the roadsides seem more like a garden than a national park. (In fact, many of the azaleas and mountains laurels along Skyline Drive were planted in the 1930s, though the species are natives.) The Limberlost Trail is an excellent place to enjoy these shrubs, which are only a small part of the park's list of more than 800 species of wildflowers.

In fall, just about the time the goldenrods and asters are winding down the year's wildflower show, the park's hardwood trees begin their annual spectacle. Maples, oaks, hickories, blackgums, tuliptrees, and other species turn every shade from yellow through rust and orange to brilliant scarlet.

The landscape within Shenandoah National Park is dominated by the Blue Ridge range of the Appalachian Mountains, ancient uplands that once rose far higher but have been worn down by eons of erosion. The bluish haze of water vapor that sometimes hovers over the forests gave the range its name.

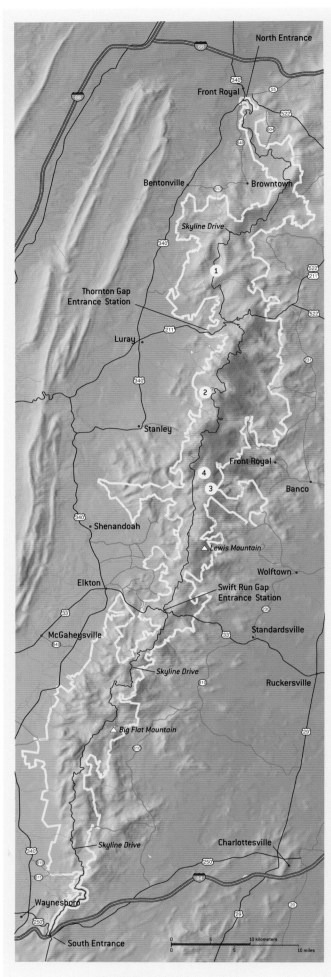

SHENANDOAH WESTERN VIRGINIA

AREA
197,438 acres (799 sq km)
ESTABLISHED
December 1935
VISITOR INFORMATION
(540) 999 3500;
www.nps.gov/shen

KEY ATTRACTIONS ① Skyline
Drive ② Skyland
③ Rapidan Camp ④ Dark
Hollow Falls
NOTABLE WILDLIFE black bear,
white-tailed deer, gray fox,
peregrine falcon, wild turkey

Beautiful Dark Hollow Falls was once admired by Virginia native
Thomas Jefferson. Located in the Big Meadows area, the 70-foot-high
waterfall is among the park's most impressive and easiest to visit,
reached by a 0.7-mile trail. Black bears are sometimes seen nearby.

The Appalachians are renowned for their fall foliage display, and Shenandoah National Park quite possibly claims top honors within the entire range.

Spring is the best time to enjoy the park's many waterfalls, including 70-foot-high Dark Hollow Falls, a superb cascade to which President Thomas Jefferson once made a visit. Among other waterfalls are Whiteoak Falls, Jones Run Falls, and Doyles River Falls, some dropping more than 80 feet. None of Shenandoah's waterfalls is visible from Skyline Drive, and some require fairly strenuous hikes for viewing.

By the time Shenandoah National Park was authorized by Congress in the 1920s, hundreds of families had long been living in this part of the then remote Appalachians. Nearly all had moved away by the time the park was established in 1935, though traces of old communities can be seen throughout the area: log cabins, stone walls, orchards, cemeteries, and other artifacts. Park visitors can also take a ranger-led van tour to Rapidan Camp, which served as the "summer White House" for President Herbert Hoover in 1931. The cabin where President and Mrs Hoover stayed has been restored to its period appearance.

Among the attractions within the park is the Skyland Resort, including a lodge dating from the 1890s. The development was built in 1895 as a place where the wealthy would come to relax and recreate. Skyland is located near the highest point on Skyline Drive, at 3,680 feet in elevation. A 1.6-mile round-trip hike nearby leads to the top of Stony Man, at 4,010 feet the second-highest summit in the park. The views from the top are as grand as they are far-reaching.

Although the most commonly seen large mammal in Shenandoah is the white-tailed deer, the park is home to a large population of black bears, which are occasionally spotted even by motorists on Skyline Drive. Around 40 percent of Shenandoah National Park is officially designated wilderness, and hikers are generally free to camp wherever they like, after obtaining a free permit. Backcountry campers need to learn and follow rules for food storage and other safety precautions to avoid encounters with bears. Most of the park comprises hardwood forest, but conifers such as balsam fir and red spruce grow at higher elevations. As a result, birds such as brown creeper and Blackburnian warbler nest here, much farther south than their normal northern range.

Shenandoah National Park provides a home for more than 50 species of mammals. Among the most frequently seen are white-tailed deer, which browse along roadsides at dawn and dusk. More than 200 species of resident and migratory birds have been sighted, evidence of the park's varied natural habitats.

Fall finds motorists enjoying the spectacle of colorful foliage along the park's 105-mile Skyline Drive. Oaks, hickories, maples, and other hardwoods create stunning scenes painted in a natural palette of yellow, red, and orange. Seventy-five overlooks are located along this famed scenic route.

GREAT SMOKY MOUNTAINS NATIONAL PARK

THE MOST VISITED NATIONAL PARK IN THE United States, Great Smoky Mountains each year attracts millions of visitors who marvel at its panoramas of mountains and forest, who hike trails through lush hardwood coves and along ridges, and who picnic, fish, take photographs, and find many other ways to enjoy its attractions.

Yet scientists know there is much more to Great Smoky Mountains National Park than beauty and recreation, as appealing as they are. The Smokies, a part of the long chain of the Appalachian Mountains, have the greatest biological diversity of any similarly sized area in the world outside the tropics. And what does this mean to the non-scientist visitor? A long list of

wildlife, from elk and black bears to rare salamanders, and an even longer list of trees, shrubs, and other plants, including fabulous displays of wildflowers through much of the year.

A combination of circumstances contribute to this unparalleled biodiversity. The Great Smokies are ancient mountains, once standing far higher than they rise today but worn by hundreds of millions of years of erosion. They have been relatively untouched by events such as ocean rises and ice ages, allowing flora and fauna to endure and diversify. The mountains receive enough rain for the habitat to be classified as a temperate rainforest, and the elevation range—from 875 to 6,643 feet—means that in one day a park visitor can experience environments equivalent to those of Georgia to the south and Canada to the north.

In addition, about one-quarter of the park's woodland is composed of old-growth deciduous forest, making it one of the most significant areas of mature hardwood forest on the continent. For the biologist, this means the park offers a secure home to species that are rare elsewhere. For the traveler, it means the opportunity to admire magnificent specimens of dozens of species of trees such as white oak, tuliptree, blackgum, and beech.

Newfound Gap Road crosses the park and the crest of the Great Smoky Mountains from west to east, ascending around 3,000 feet as it connects the Sugarlands Visitor Center in Tennessee and the Oconaluftee Visitor Center in North Carolina. Many scenic overlooks along the way offer spectacular views of mountain crests and valleys,

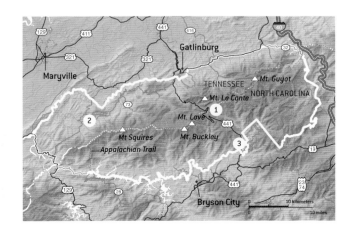

GREAT SMOKY MOUNTAINS
TENNESSEE AND NORTH CAROLINA

AREA
521,086 acres (2,109 sq km)

ESTABLISHED
1934

VISITOR INFORMATION
(865) 436 1200;
www.nps.gov/grsm

KEY ATTRACTIONS ① Newfound Gap Road ② Cades Cove ③ Mountain Farm Museum

NOTABLE WILDLIFE Black bear, elk, white-tailed deer, red squirrel, more than 30 species of salamander

as well as rock formations such as Chimney Tops, a double-summit formation of bare rock that has long been a local landmark.

By the time the road reaches 5,046-foot Newfound Gap, the traveler has passed through several life zones: cove hardwood, pine-oak, northern hardwood, and spruce-fir vegetation. Near the gap (a low point in a mountain ridge), a side road leads to 6,643-foot Clingmans Dome, with an observation tower from which, on a clear day, the view can take in seven states.

Newfound Gap Road's eastern end lies near the Mountain Farm Museum, where authentic Appalachian buildings such as a blacksmith shop, log house, and barn have been gathered to re-create a 19th-century community. Nearby stands Mingus Mill, built in 1886 to grind corn and other grains.

Nature and history also form a compelling combination at Cades Cove, a beautiful area in the northwestern part of the park that is one of Great Smoky Mountains' most popular destinations. An 11-mile loop road passes through woodland and meadows where wildflowers abound. There are frequent sightings of wildlife such as white-tailed deer and wild turkey. This is one of the best places to spot a black bear, a species that numbers around 1,500 in the park, or two per square mile. Here, too, stand historic buildings such as houses, churches, and a gristmill.

Far less crowded than Cades Cove, the Cataloochee area at the park's eastern border preserves the quaint, pastoral setting

Around 1,500 black bears inhabit the park, making Great Smoky Mountains one of the most important population centers for this mammal in the eastern United States. Around 85 percent of a bear's diet is composed of plant material such as berries and nuts, and males of more than 600 pounds have been documented in the park.

Harsh climate conditions make life a struggle for trees on 6,643-foot Clingmans Dome, the highest point in Great Smoky Mountains National Park and the third-tallest summit east of the Mississippi River. The park boasts 16 peaks rising more than 5,000 feet, while its lowest point is only 875 feet.

The red salamander is one of more than 30 salamander species found in the park. With the Earth's greatest variety of these small amphibians, Great Smoky Mountains has been called the "salamander capital of the world." Some of the park's species are found only in the southern Appalachians.

of a small local community dating from the 19th century. Cataloochee is also a very likely spot for seeing elk, a species that was extirpated from the region but has been reintroduced. These magnificent animals can weigh 700 pounds and stand 5 feet high at the shoulder.

With more than 80 inches of rain annually in the high country, plus a rugged landscape with significant elevation change, Great Smoky Mountains National Park abounds in waterfalls, from spectacular multi-level cascades rushing down steep cliffs to frothing creeks dropping over small rock ledges. Some, such as Meigs Falls and Toms Branch Falls, can be reached by road or short, easy trails. To see Ramsey Cascades, the park's tallest at more than 100 feet, requires a strenuous 8-mile round-trip hike; the reward is a view of the many-tiered waterfall, which splits and reforms as it drops over large rock outcrops. A moderately difficult 5-mile hike leads to Abrams Falls, which,

though only 20 feet high, is among the park's most spectacular waterfalls, with a voluminous creek crashing over a ledge into a large pool at the base.

Though not so viscerally powerful as waterfalls, the flowering plants of Great Smoky Mountains National Park offer rewards just as satisfying. They are so diverse and abundant that some rangers have nicknamed this "Wildflower National Park." With more than 1,660 species of flowering plants, Great Smoky Mountains boasts more varieties than any other national park in North America. Some of the most eye-catching are mountain laurel, catawba and rosebay rhododendrons, flame azalea, flowering dogwood, and Fraser magnolia, but smaller varieties such as trilliums, lady's-slipper orchids, and columbine are just as colorful. For its biological diversity alone, Great Smoky Mountains deserves its place as the most popular national park.

MAMMOTH CAVE NATIONAL PARK

BENEATH THE HARDWOOD FORESTS AND meandering streams of central Kentucky lies the world's longest cave system, a place of arena-sized rooms, near-endless labyrinthine passageways, bizarre and beautiful formations, underground rivers, and rare life-forms.

So lengthy are the passages of Mammoth Cave—more than 365 miles have been mapped by explorers, with hundreds more believed to exist—that if the world's second- and third-longest caves were combined, Mammoth would still be more than 100 miles longer. Yet the name "Mammoth" was applied in the 19th century not because of that fact, but to acknowledge the immense size of the cave's underground chambers. At one time, bands played for dancing in rooms near the entrance, with plenty of space left over for tables.

Native Americans once ranged miles into the cave to gather minerals, and today's visitors can still walk into Mammoth Cave via the Historic Entrance. Tours pass into the huge Rotunda and beyond to enjoy sites with colorful names such as Giant's Coffin, Bottomless Pit, Fat Man's Misery, and Mammoth Dome. Other tours visit places such as Frozen Niagara, an extraordinary conglomeration of flowstones (sheetlike deposits of calcite formed where water has flowed down the walls and along the floors of the cave); the Snowball Room with its gypsum ceiling; and the below-ground rivers that are still carving passages.

Some tours operate by lantern light, so visitors can experience the cave the way tourists did in the mid-19th century. For truly adventurous visitors, rangers lead a Wild Cave Tour that

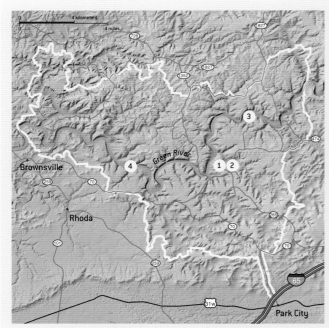

MAMMOTH CAVE CENTRAL KENTUCKY

AREA
52,839 acres (214 sq km)

ESTABLISHED
July 1941

VISITOR INFORMATION
(270) 758 2180;
www.nps.gov/maca

KEY ATTRACTIONS ① Historic
Entrance ② The Rotunda
③ Great Onyx Cave
④ Green River

NOTABLE WILDLIFE White-tailed
deer, several bat species,
wild turkey

requires climbing steep walls, crawling over rough rock, and squeezing through constricted passages in areas off the developed tour routes.

Much of Mammoth is a "dry" cave, where impermeable rock overhead repels the dripping water that creates speleothems (cave formations). Yet other areas offer a fantastic array of stalactites, stalagmites, helictites (formations with a curving or angular, rather than vertical, form), travertine dams, and gypsum "flowers" in an infinite variety of shapes and sizes. Some of the most striking formations are found in a separate cavern called Great Onyx Cave, which operated as a private tourist attraction until the 1960s and is now visited on tours led by park rangers carrying lanterns. Formations such as the evocative Nativity inspired an early tourism promotion to call Onyx Cave "a fairyland of delight," a description that remains apt.

While Mammoth Cave ranks as one of the world's natural wonders, visitors to the national park should not neglect its attractions on the surface. Canoeing or kayaking along the Green and Nolin Rivers offers a quiet escape into the Kentucky woodland environment. Camping is allowed on river islands and sandbars, where boaters can enjoy the night sky and the hoots of owls far from the crowds around the cave.

Cavers such as these in the New Discovery area have explored more than 365 miles of passages within Mammoth Cave, making this the world's longest cave system. Determined cavers continue to crawl through constricted passageways to find new corridors, adding lines to Mammoth Cave's convoluted map.

CONGAREE NATIONAL PARK

A VISIT TO CONGAREE NATIONAL PARK IS like traveling back to an earlier America: a time and place of awesomely tall trees, where the loudest sound is the laughing cry of a pileated woodpecker and the seasons are marked not by the calendar but by the rise and fall of rivers. The forest here possesses an almost tropical lushness, with the "knees" of bald-cypresses rising from the water and strands of Spanish moss hanging from tree limbs. In spring, Congaree is a picture painted with every imaginable shade of green.

Congaree protects the largest remaining area of old-growth floodplain forest in the United States. Saved from most logging by its difficult access—large areas of what is now the park are flooded for much of the year—it is a place where oaks, sweetgums, bald-cypresses, and loblolly pines rise high into the sky, with an average canopy height of more than 100 feet. The park boasts several trees so big that they rank as national or state champions of their species or variety, including a loblolly pine 167 feet high—the tallest in the country.

Formerly a national monument, Congaree is one of the nation's newest national parks, having achieved that designation in 2003. Facilities are few, comprising a fine visitor center, a boardwalk trail, more than 20 miles of hiking routes, and primitive campsites. Most of the park is designated wilderness, accessible only on foot or by canoe or kayak.

Boating is one of the best ways to experience Congaree, paddling quietly along tree-shaded waterways, enjoying the sights and sounds of a near-primeval southern bottomland forest. Otters play on riverbanks, raccoons peer down from branches, and the loud hoots of barred owls ring out through the trees. A marked canoe trail passes through the park, and rangers lead guided boat trips on most weekends.

Beginning at the visitor center, a 2.4-mile elevated boardwalk winds through the forest, offering close views of flora and fauna, from tiny, camouflaged tree frogs to the brilliant

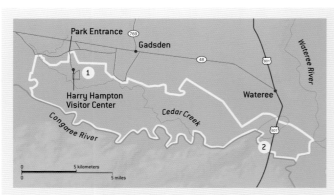

CONGAREE SOUTH CAROLINA

AREA
24,336 acres (98 sq km)
ESTABLISHED
November 2003
VISITOR INFORMATION
(803) 776 4396;
www.nps.gov/cosw

KEY ATTRACTIONS ① Boardwalk
trail ② canoe trail
NOTABLE WILDLIFE White-tailed
deer, pileated woodpecker, barred
owl, river otter

The country's largest expanse of old-growth bottomland hardwood forest is protected within Congaree National Park, where trees such as bald-cypress, water tupelo, sweetgum, and loblolly pine tower over often flooded lowland. Canoeing or kayaking are often the best ways to explore this wilderness.

Giving its distinctive "Who cooks for you?" call, the barred owl is one of the most common birds of southern swamps—although it is heard far more often than it is seen. Ragged edges on wing feathers help it fly silently as it swoops down to capture small mammals, birds, reptiles, and amphibians.

golden prothonotary warbler. Red-shouldered hawks soar overhead, giving high-pitched screams, and wood ducks, among the world's most beautiful waterfowl, swim silently among the bald-cypress knees.

Hiking trails loop through backcountry areas of Congaree, providing access to both mature forest and tracts that were logged in the mid-20th century. The varying age of the forest increases the diversity of resident wildlife. Among the tallest trees in the park's backcountry are cherrybark oak and sweetgum, with individuals of both species topping 150 feet. Trails can be muddy or even flooded at times, but lucky hikers are occasionally rewarded with views of wild turkey, bobcats, Swainson's warblers, or other seldom seen creatures.

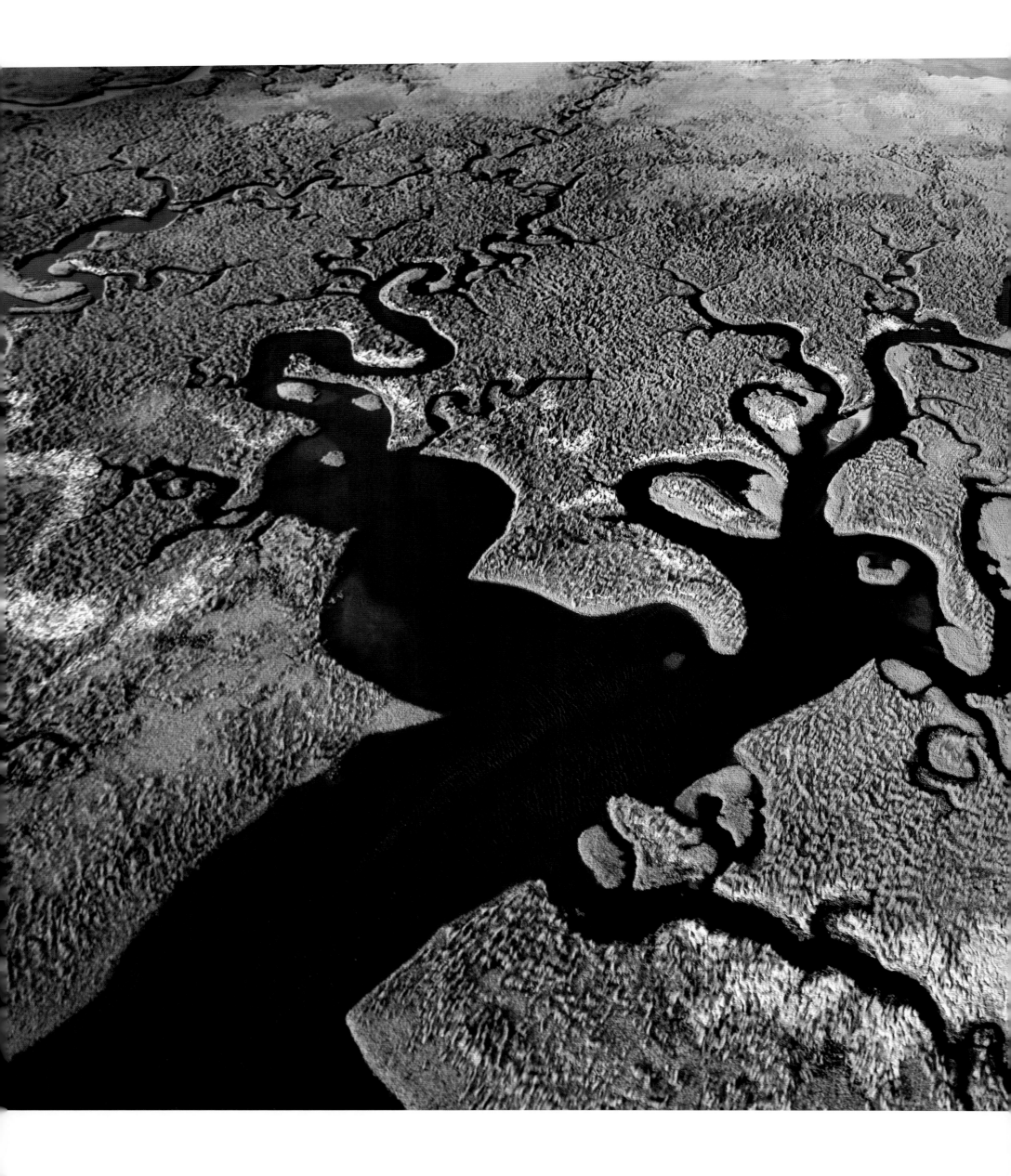

EVERGLADES NATIONAL PARK

A VAST AND MOSTLY UNTRACKED "river of grass," Florida's Everglades National Park comprises an ecosystem unique in North America, and indeed in the world. Covering much of the southern tip of peninsular Florida, the Everglades is an enormous puzzle whose various parts include fresh and brackish marshes, hardwood and conifer woodlands, wet and dry prairies, ponds, rivers, and an expanse of saltwater bay. By any measurement, the Everglades ranks with the planet's most important natural areas.

Before humans altered the environment, the Everglades ecosystem functioned on cycles determined by the flow of water. Fed by summer rains, a broad sheet of water flowed south from central Florida across the Everglades to the sea, nourishing thousands of species of plants and animals. Highways, agriculture, and suburbs have impeded that flow, starving the Everglades of much of the water it needs to sustain itself. As a result, southern Florida is now the focus of the largest environmental-restoration project in history, as scientists and engineers attempt to rebuild an ecosystem that has sustained significant damage.

Despite its troubled recent history, Everglades National Park remains an immensely rewarding place to visit. Its importance can be judged by the fact that it has been designated a World Heritage Site, an International Biosphere Reserve, and a Wetland of International Importance. Flocks of beautiful wading birds fly overhead, while alligators bask beside waterways where bald eagles nest. A few endangered Florida panthers stalk wooded areas, hoping to track white-tailed deer.

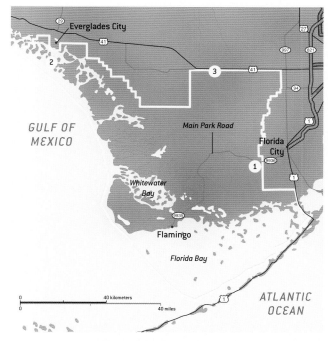

EVERGLADES SOUTHERN FLORIDA

AREA
1,506,000 acres (6,095 sq km)
ESTABLISHED
December 1947
VISITOR INFORMATION
(305) 242 7700;
www.nps.gov/ever

KEY ATTRACTIONS ① Royal Palm
② Ten Thousand Islands
③ Shark Valley
NOTABLE WILDLIFE American alligator, American crocodile, indigo snake, Florida panther, West Indian manatee, wood stork

A place as much of water as of land, Everglades National Park operates on seasonal cycles of flooding and drying, its flora and fauna adapted to annual rainfall patterns. Although near the sprawling metropolis of Miami, the park encompasses some of the wildest and most remote backcountry in the eastern United States.

More than 360 species of birds, more than 40 species of mammals, and more than 50 species of reptiles have been found within the park. Yet these are only the most visible of the park's fauna, which comprises hundreds of species of fish, amphibians, and insects and other invertebrates.

Just inside the park's eastern entrance, the Ernest Coe Visitor Center features exhibits and films that provide an introduction to the Everglades. A short distance farther, the Royal Palm Center offers two of the park's most popular trails. The easy half-mile Anhinga Trail follows a boardwalk through a sawgrass marsh where alligators are easily seen and photographed. Among the many waterbirds that might be seen from the trail are anhingas, sometimes called "snakebirds" for the way they swim with only their long, sinuous necks above water. The adjacent half-mile Gumbo Limbo Trail passes through a lush subtropical hammock (a grove of hardwood trees) studded with graceful royal palms and gumbo limbos, trees with distinctive peeling bark.

The main park road continues past the Royal Palm Center through dry grassland with scattered slash pines and wetter grassland with bald-cypresses, reaching a turn-off at the Pahayokee Overlook. Here a short boardwalk leads to an observation platform with far-reaching views over the seasonally flooded "river of grass" that is the heart of the Everglades. Because this landscape is so flat—elevations within the entire park range just a few feet above sea level—differences of 1 foot can mean a change in habitat. This is apparent at the next trail along the road, the Mahogany Hammock Trail, where slightly higher ground supports a verdant growth of hardwood trees, including the largest mahogany tree in the United States.

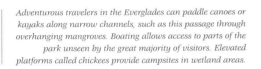
Adventurous travelers in the Everglades can paddle canoes or kayaks along narrow channels, such as this passage through overhanging mangroves. Boating allows access to parts of the park unseen by the great majority of visitors. Elevated platforms called chickees provide campsites in wetland areas.

Great egrets were once killed for their long back plumes, which were used to decorate women's hats in the 19th century. Today they and other wading birds such as snowy egrets, roseate spoonbills, and wood storks face new dangers in the form of habitat loss and environmental degradation.

The road ends at Flamingo, on Florida Bay, where views from the shore take in an array of islands scattered across the blue water. Kayaking is a popular activity here, paddling out to explore this paradisiacal seascape. American crocodiles, a threatened species, sometimes sun themselves on mudflats, while flocks of gorgeous roseate spoonbills feed in the shallows. Small numbers of flamingos occasionally take up residence near the community of Flamingo, using their weirdly shaped downcurved bills to feed on tiny water creatures.

The northern part of Everglades National Park is reached by a separate entrance at the Shark Valley area. A 15-mile loop road leads south, deep into the grassland. Closed to private vehicles, this road can be toured on a tram ride narrated by a park ranger. An even more intimate way to explore the area is by bicycle, which can be rented at Shark Valley. This is a fine place to look for snail kite, a small, threatened type of hawk that feeds almost exclusively on large apple snails.

An observation tower at the southern end of the loop road provides the best panoramic view within the park: its 65-foot-high viewpoint is the tallest for many miles in any direction. From here, the magnificent wilderness scene below seems more like an ocean of grass than a river.

The park's third main entry point is the Gulf Coast Visitor Center at Everglades City, in the northwestern corner of the park. This is the gateway to the Ten Thousand Islands, a maze of narrow waterways winding among countless small islands, comprising the largest area of protected mangrove forest in the western hemisphere. Guided boat tours are offered here, although many visitors prefer to rent a canoe or kayak and explore on their own.

Truly adventurous boaters can take on the famed Wilderness Waterway, a 99-mile trip from Everglades City to Flamingo. Usually requiring around nine days to paddle, this adventure means camping on elevated platforms called chickees, and is recommended for experienced boaters only. Yet even moderately skilled boaters can enjoy day trips around this wonderland of green islands and blue water. Lucky paddlers might see a West Indian manatee, the appealingly homely "sea cow" that frequents shallow water around southern Florida coasts.

Whether by vehicle, boat, or trail, visitors will find endless diversity within Everglades National Park, protecting the largest wilderness area east of the Mississippi River and a virtual kaleidoscope of wildlife. As environmental restoration work continues, visitors can feel more secure that this vitally important habitat—with its panthers, water birds, alligators, crocodiles, and manatees—will endure as a preserve for the best of southern Florida's nature.

Once an endangered species, the American alligator has made a comeback and is now common in much of the southeastern United States. Although alligators can pose a threat to humans, most visitors will be much more preoccupied with avoiding a different animal: the mosquito.

BISCAYNE NATIONAL PARK

STANDING ON THE SHORE OF FLORIDA'S Biscayne Bay at Convoy Point, a visitor can experience some of the beauty of Biscayne National Park. The blue water glistens in the sun, emerald-green islands dot the bay, and sea birds wheel through the air. Yet those who keep their feet on dry land will never appreciate all that this unique park has to offer. With water making up 95 percent of its area, Biscayne most fully rewards those who venture into the bay by boat or—better yet—enter the water to snorkel or dive and see its underwater spectacle up close.

Four distinct ecosystems compose Biscayne National Park: a fringe of mangrove forest on the mainland, a portion of Biscayne Bay, the northernmost of the famed Florida Keys (a chain of islands made of coral rock), and the northernmost coral reefs in the United States. Of these, the coral reef environment offers the greatest range of beauty, with fish and invertebrates in such colors it seems that someone spilled a jewel box into the water. The coral itself, made up of countless numbers of tiny animals and their self-constructed homes, grows in a fantastic multitude of shapes, from branches to fans to rounded mounds.

Visitors with boats and gear can access the reef on their own; others can take concessioner-operated tours from Convoy Point 10 miles out to the reef. Those who do not want to get wet can ride on a glass-bottom boat, through the hull of which sights might include some of the hundreds of species of fish found in the bay. Other boats take snorkelers and divers to the reef for a few hours of exploring the spectacularly diverse array of life below the surface. Divers, snorkelers, or boaters might well have the thrill of spotting a sea turtle swimming through the clear waters of Biscayne Bay. Three species of sea turtles are seen with varying degrees of regularity in the park, and two others have been recorded here. All are federally listed as threatened or endangered.

Kayaks and canoes can also be brought to the park or rented to explore the mangrove forest around Convoy Point, where trees rise above the water's surface on stilt-like roots. Some kayakers and canoeists make their way to Elliott Key or Boca Chita Key (either by paddling across Biscayne Bay or being transported by a larger boat) for primitive camping. The environments of mangrove shore, wooded keys, beaches, and near-shore shallow water provide homes for many species of birds such as egrets, pelicans, and terns. The endangered West Indian manatee is sometimes seen near shore. Biscayne National Park is known as home for the critically endangered Schaus' swallowtail butterfly, which in the 1980s had been reduced to fewer than 100 individuals.

Narrow channels among the islands immerse boaters in a subtropical wilderness of dense vegetation and wildlife that may include sharks, rays, flocks of wading birds, jellyfish, spiny lobsters, and dozens more species. Paddling among these beautiful islands, it is hard to imagine that the metropolis of Miami is less than 30 miles away.

Fishing ranks among the most popular park activities, with anglers going after species such as grouper, sea trout, wahoo, snapper, hogfish, and tuna. Spiny lobster and blue and stone crab can also be harvested seasonally, providing many a delicious dinner for those successful in their efforts. Part of the

More than 500 species of fish have been documented within Biscayne, from sharks to stingrays to brightly colored parrotfish, damselfish, and angelfish. Divers and snorkelers can admire this rainbow of sea life against a background of invertebrate animals such as sea fans and brain and elkhorn coral.

West Indian manatees, such as this nursing mother and calf, are sometimes seen in the shallow coastal waters of Biscayne National Park.

BISCAYNE FLORIDA

AREA
172,971 acres (700 sq km)
ESTABLISHED
June 1980
VISITOR INFORMATION
(305) 230 7275;
www.nps.gov/bisc

KEY ATTRACTIONS ① Convoy Point
② Elliott Key ③ Boca Chita Key
NOTABLE WILDLIFE West Indian
manatee, Schaus' swallowtail
butterfly, American crocodile, five
species of sea turtle, more than
500 species of fish

The hawksbill is one of three species of sea turtles seen commonly in Biscayne National Park, along with green and loggerhead. Park rangers monitor beaches during nesting season to protect eggs from raccoons and other predators, as well as disturbance by humans.

park lies within the Biscayne Bay-Card Sound Lobster
Sanctuary, a zone set aside to provide a no-harvest refuge for
spiny lobsters, assuring that the crustacean will maintain a
healthy population in the future.

Although nature ranks as the highlight of a trip to Biscayne
National Park, its human history is equally fascinating. Most
islands in the park show evidence of the Native Americans who
lived here thousands of years ago, harvesting conch, whelk,
and other sea creatures. Encompassed within the park, too, are
the remnants of the odd over-water community called
Stiltsville, once a notorious place of nightclubs and illegal
gambling that saw frequent police raids. Adams Key, now open
to picnicking and hiking, was home to the Cocolobo Club, a
millionaire's getaway that hosted several presidents. Businessman
Mark Honeywell once owned part of Boca Chita Key. The 65-
foot ornamental lighthouse he built there in the 1930s offers
one of the best views of Biscayne Bay and the Miami skyline.

Unique in the National Park Service, Biscayne's Marine
Heritage Trail guides divers in exploring some of the more than
three dozen shipwrecks that lie below the surface of Biscayne
Bay. Among them are an iron-hulled steamship that sank in
1878 en route to Havana, a three-masted ship that ran aground
in 1905, and a steel-hulled schooner that sank in 1966.

DRY TORTUGAS NATIONAL PARK

S ET IN SUPERB SOLITUDE AMID THE BLUE water of the Gulf of Mexico, Dry Tortugas National Park offers a fascinating union of history and nature—a combination with rewards greatly disproportionate to the seven small islands that make up its land area.

The adventure begins even before arrival at the park itself. Dry Tortugas is accessible only by boat or float plane, and during the 70-mile trip from Key West, visitors may well spot sea turtles, sharks, rays, large fish, or dolphins—the water is so clear that sea life is visible from a passenger ferry or from the air.

On arrival at the main island of Garden Key, all attention turns to the imposing sight of Fort Jefferson, built as a U.S. Army post in the mid-19th century. Constructed of 16 million bricks, it is so large that a walk around the top of its exterior walls requires a half-mile hike. Although it was never attacked, Fort Jefferson played supporting roles in the Civil War and the Spanish-American War, and at one time was home to nearly 2,000 residents. Fort Jefferson also served for a time as a prison. Its most famous inmate was Dr. Samuel Mudd, who was convicted of conspiracy for setting the broken leg of John Wilkes Booth, the assassin of President Abraham Lincoln.

The water around Garden Key abounds with corals, starfish, conchs, sea turtles, rays, and an assortment of fish in almost every color of the spectrum. Some of these can be seen simply by walking around the moat that surrounds Fort Jefferson, but many more are visible to those who go snorkeling in the crystalline water.

The skies around Garden Key are full of life, as well. Each year, hundreds of birdwatchers make the journey to this remote park

DRY TORTUGAS FLORIDA

AREA
64,701 acres (262 sq km)
ESTABLISHED
October 1992
VISITOR INFORMATION
(305) 242 7700;
www.nps.gov/drto

KEY ATTRACTIONS ① Fort
Jefferson ② Garden Key
③ Bush Key
NOTABLE WILDLIFE Sea turtles,
sooty tern, brown noddy,
magnificent frigatebird

Activities at Dry Tortugas National Park center on massive Fort Jefferson, begun as a U.S. Army post in 1846 and never officially completed. Built on Garden Key of 16 million bricks, it never saw direct action in wartime. Adjacent Bush Key is an important breeding ground for thousands of terns.

Magnificent frigatebirds are among the many species that attract birdwatchers to the Dry Tortugas. Adult males of this predatory seabird have brilliant scarlet throat pouches, which they inflate and shake to attract females.

Although most visitors to Fort Jefferson make day trips (boats and seaplanes provide the only access), primitive camping is allowed on Garden Key. Overnight stays allow visitors to experience the beautiful sunsets for which the Gulf of Mexico is known.

to see species such as terns (a large breeding colony of sooty terns and brown noddies is located on nearby Bush Key), white-tailed tropicbirds, magnificent frigatebirds, brown and masked boobies, and dozens of other species. In spring, astounding numbers of birds migrating northward across the Caribbean stop to rest at Garden Key, creating a breathtaking spectacle in which birds crowd every tree, shrub, and patch of grass on the island.

Although the boundaries of Dry Tortugas National Park encompass more than 100 square miles, its seven small islands make up less than 1 percent of the area. Visiting most islands requires a private boat. Strict rules protect the environment of much of the surrounding Gulf of Mexico, providing a safe haven for endangered sea turtles as well as many species of fish that are declining in the region.

VIRGIN ISLANDS NATIONAL PARK

VIRGIN ISLANDS NATIONAL PARK BEAUTIFULLY exemplifies the things that draw travelers to the Caribbean: beaches of pale golden sand, warm water of intense blue-green, and abundant sunshine. Visitors intent on a few lazy days of swimming, sunbathing, and generally relaxing will find a virtual paradise on the small tropical island of Saint John, a part of the territory of the United States Virgin Islands. Saint John's status as a getaway is enhanced by the fact that, unlike most Caribbean vacation islands, it is accessible only by boat.

Saint John's beauty attracted many wealthy people to build holiday homes on the island in the early 20th century. One of them, philanthropist Laurance Rockefeller, was among those who worried that development would spoil the island. Rockefeller helped lead efforts to acquire land and create a national park. Today, more than half of Saint John lies within Virgin Islands National Park, which also includes undeveloped Hessell Island, located off nearby Saint Thomas Island. Park protection assures that most of Saint John will remain unspoiled, free of resorts and other businesses, and open to public enjoyment.

For many visitors, the most rewarding part of Virgin Islands National Park lies offshore, around the coral reefs that border parts of Saint John. Trunk Bay is renowned as one of the world's most beautiful beaches, a long arc of sand named for the loggerhead sea turtles that early settlers thought resembled a trunk. Yet, attractive as the bay is, snorkelers and divers will find an even more fantastic undersea world in its waters. More than 500 species of fish have been identified around the Virgin Islands, and dozens of kinds might be seen swimming around a coral reef, including barracudas, butterflyfish, groupers, eels, and angelfish. Other reef residents include sea turtles, rays, lobsters, seastars, and anemones. An underwater snorkeling trail, complete with interpretive signs, lies offshore from Trunk Bay.

Other beautiful beaches are located at Hawksnest Bay, Cinnamon Bay, and Maho Bay, with varying levels of amenities such as dining and gear rental for activities like kayaking and windsurfing.

Elsewhere on Saint John, visitors enjoy fantastic views from various overlooks along the island's hilly roads. On the northern part of the island are the ruins of the historic Annaberg sugar mill, dating from the 18th century when enslaved workers cultivated sugar cane as the island's major industry. Hundreds of structures from the sugar era dot the island, including windmills, boiling houses, workers' houses, and cemeteries. Costumed interpreters give regular living-history exhibitions at Annaberg.

Visitors can explore Saint John on 20 park hiking trails, some of which lead to remote swimming and snorkeling beaches, abandoned sugar plantations, and petroglyphs (rock carvings) created by the Taino people, who were inhabiting the island when Christopher Columbus reached the Caribbean in 1492. Several park trails ascend hills for spectacular panoramic vistas overlooking the sea and nearby islands.

VIRGIN ISLANDS SAINT JOHN, U.S. VIRGIN ISLANDS

AREA
14,686 acres (59 sq km)
ESTABLISHED
August 1956
VISITOR INFORMATION
(340) 776 6201;
www.nps.gov/viis

KEY ATTRACTIONS ① Trunk Bay
② Cinnamon Bay ③ Annaberg Plantation
NOTABLE WILDLIFE Sea turtles, 500 species of tropical fish, brown pelican, magnificent frigatebird, brown booby

Gorgeous sandy beaches like this one at Hawksnest Bay create idyllic scenes for beachgoers on Saint John. With more than half this small island lying within Virgin Islands National Park, Saint John offers visitors coasts, hills, and trails in large part untouched by tourism development.

Just offshore at Trunk Bay is a 225-yard-long self-guided snorkeling trail, with underwater signs interpreting the life of a coral reef. More than 300 species of fish have been identified in Saint John's waters, many of them displaying brilliant colors.

HOT SPRINGS
NATIONAL PARK

PERHAPS AMERICA'S MOST UNUSUAL national park, Hot Springs offers visitors a chance to immerse themselves in a fascinating historic site set in the rugged Ouachita Mountains of western Arkansas. That history includes the establishment of a federal protected area at Hot Springs in 1832, making it the oldest unit within the present National Park Service. In the decades since, a city has grown up around the springs, creating a unique juxtaposition of national park and urban area.

Stories of soothing hot springs in a Ouachita Mountain valley were heard by French explorers of the 18th century. By the early 19th century, after the region was acquired by the United States in the 1803 Louisiana Purchase, a small community had grown up around the springs to serve those bathing in the "healing" waters. The 1832 reservation was designated to protect what was then considered an important national health resource.

Although the springs were mysterious to those first settlers, scientists now know that rainwater penetrates about a mile deep into the Earth, where it is heated by natural geological processes, returns to the surface (after around 4,000 years), and flows from springs at a temperature of 143°F (62°C) and at a rate of 700,000 gallons a day.

Over the years, elaborate bathhouses were built to serve visitors, and nearly all the spring water was collected and piped to bathhouses and hotels. The eight imposing structures standing along Bathhouse Row National Historic Landmark District are the centerpiece of the park. The three-story Fordyce Bathhouse now serves as a museum and visitor center, showcasing the elaborately beautiful architectural amenities provided for bathers when it opened in 1915: two courtyards, marble walls and staircases, terracotta fountains, and a spectacularly colorful stained-glass ceiling, as well as a bowling

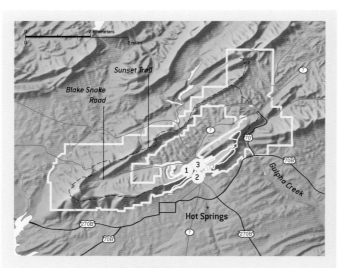

HOT SPRINGS ARKANSAS

AREA
5,550 acres (22 sq km)
ESTABLISHED
March 1921
VISITOR INFORMATION
(501) 620 6715;
www.nps.gov/hosp

KEY ATTRACTIONS ① Bathhouse Row ② Fordyce Bathhouse ③ Grand Promenade
NOTABLE WILDLIFE White-tailed deer, raccoon, pileated woodpecker

Gulpha Creek flows through Hot Springs National Park, where trails wind up and down ridges of the Ouachita Mountains. Forests of oak, hickory, and pine include some very large specimens of shortleaf pine, long protected within the oldest unit of the National Park Service.

Away from the draws of Bathhouse Row, the lush creek valleys of Hot Springs National Park support numerous species of amphibians, including salamanders, frogs, treefrogs, and toads, including the eastern spadefoot toad, which spends much of its time buried in sandy soil.

Elaborate decorative elements on the Fordyce Bathhouse remind visitors of the glory days of spas, when the rich and famous traveled to Hot Springs to "take the waters," and several major-league baseball teams conducted spring training here. Today the Fordyce serves as the park visitor center.

alley, gymnasiums, private treatment rooms, and a roof garden. In the early 20th century, when the popularity of resort spas and public baths was at its peak, Hot Springs hosted wealthy families, politicians, famous athletes, and even notorious gangsters, all of whom came to soak in its waters. Most bathhouses have closed since then, but traditional baths and spa treatments are still available at the 1912 Buckstaff Bathhouse and at local hotels.

A broad brick walkway called the Grand Promenade has long been a Hot Springs highlight, offering a relaxing stroll through history, with views of the mountains that surround the city like the sides of a bowl. One nearby spring has been left in its natural state, pouring steaming water from a hillside and creating formations of tufa, or calcium carbonate deposited by the spring water.

Elsewhere in the park, 28 miles of trails wind through valleys and along hillsides densely forested with pines and hardwoods. In places along the ridges, hikers can see large outcrops of an unusual mineral called novaculite. Native Americans used it for tools, and today it is valued as the world's best sharpening stone for knives and surgical instruments. Some trails ascend the mountains surrounding the park for views of the city of Hot Springs and the historic bathhouse area.

ISLE ROYALE NATIONAL PARK

FEW PLACES IN THE LOWER 48 UNITED States offer such an exhilarating sense of remoteness as does Isle Royale National Park. Located on one large and many small islands in the northwestern part of vast Lake Superior—the largest freshwater lake in the world by surface area—it can be accessed only by boat or float plane. Isle Royale hosts fewer visitors in a year than Yellowstone National Park sees in a single day.

One reward for those who make the journey to Isle Royale is the sense of traveling centuries back in time. Despite a limited amount of development, including lodging and campgrounds, the great bulk of the park is a place of dense forests, pristine lakes, and rocky shores, where loons call, eagles soar overhead, moose feast on marsh plants, and wolves trot stealthily along trails. Almost all of its 209 square miles of land area has been federally designated wilderness since 1976.

As is the case with most of the Great Lakes country, Lake Superior and Isle Royale were shaped by glaciers. As recently as 11,000 years ago, ice lay well over a mile thick on the land. The topography of Isle Royale, including its rugged shoreline, bays, and lakes, is a result of the carving action of glaciers. Several parallel ridges run along the island, with Greenstone Ridge extending nearly the full length of Isle Royale. Long before the ice ages, the base material of Isle Royale was formed by a massive lava flow. Geological processes deposited many minerals in the Great Lakes region, including abundant copper on Isle Royale, which was used by Native Americans thousands of years ago.

Luckily for modern park visitors, low ore quality and the expense of transportation meant that commercial mines on Isle Royale ended in failure.

Hikers explore Isle Royale on more than 160 miles of trails, which meander through woodland of spruce, fir, aspen, and birch, as well as past dozens of beautiful lakes and ponds. A 40-mile trail runs along the island's "backbone," Greenstone Ridge. This trail crosses the island's high point: Mount Desor, 793 feet higher than the waters of Lake Superior. Boat transportation can be arranged to return hikers to their starting point after a one-way trek.

Kayaking is another popular activity, both on inland lakes and along the southern shore of Isle Royale. Lake Superior has notoriously bad weather at times and its

Moose exist on Isle Royale in a prey-predator relationship with gray wolves that has been long studied by biologists, who track population changes for both species. The largest member of the deer family, moose are known for the males' huge antlers, which are shed after the mating season and regrown annually.

Protected waters such as Chippewa Harbor offer fine kayaking and canoeing. Although Lake Superior can be treacherous at times, island lakes and small bays shelter boaters from wind and waves. Paddlers can access remote campsites for a true wilderness backcountry experience.

water can be rough, but Isle Royale's shoreline features many sheltered bays where paddling is safer. The national park's boundaries extend 4.5 miles along the lake surface from island coasts, and scuba divers enjoy exploring the many shipwrecks that lie beneath Lake Superior's frigid waters. Rangers lead a variety of tours from the main island Information Center at Rock Harbor.

Isle Royale is best known to naturalists for its populations of moose and gray wolves. Neither species was present when Europeans arrived in the Great Lakes region. Moose may have swum to the island a century or so ago. Wolves crossed to the island from the mainland on ice "bridges" during extremely cold winters within the past few decades. Sightings of majestic moose are not uncommon for hikers and boaters, but glimpses of wolves are much rarer. Isle Royale is one of the few national parks to close for the winter. At this season the island is snow-covered and blasted by winds, and the Lake Superior waves make boating dangerous.

ISLE ROYALE MICHIGAN

AREA
571,790 acres (2,314 sq km)

ESTABLISHED
April 1940

VISITOR INFORMATION
(906) 482 0984;
www.nps.gov/isro

KEY ATTRACTIONS
① Rock Harbor
Information Center
② Rock Harbor Lighthouse
③ Windigo Information Center

NOTABLE WILDLIFE
Gray wolf, moose, red fox,
common loon, gray jay

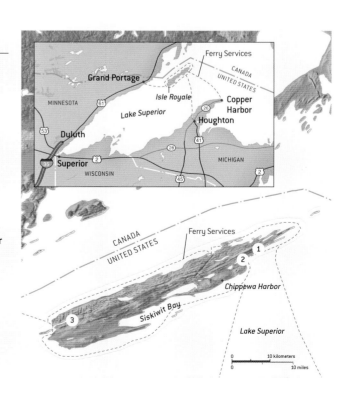

VOYAGEURS NATIONAL PARK

THE DEEP GREEN OF CONIFER FOREST AND the rich blue of lakes are the dominant colors in this wild and beautiful park on the United States–Canada border. The North Woods landscape of Voyageurs National Park recalls the era in the 18th and 19th centuries when Native Americans and French fur traders, called *voyageurs*, traveled in long birch-bark canoes, paddling for days across lakes and along rivers. The two cultures met to exchange manufactured goods for the beaver furs that were in demand for fashions of the time.

Water is still the primary mode of transportation in the park. More than one-third of Voyageurs' surface area is lake or river, and although visitor centers and some hiking trails can be reached by road, all the national park's campsites and much of its best scenery are accessible only by boat. Voyageurs encompasses 655 miles of shoreline and more than 500 islands.

In summer, hundreds of visitors take houseboats onto the park's large lakes—Rainy, Kabetogama, Namakan, and Crane—to explore the almost endless number of isolated bays and coves, for fishing or just relaxing, surrounded by woods of spruce, fir, pine, aspen, and birch. Boaters can reach sites such as Ellsworth Rock Gardens, with rock sculptures and colorful flower beds, and Grassy Bay Cliffs, where imposing walls of gray and pinkish granite rise vertically from the water. At Kettle Falls, the waterway between Rainy and Namakan Lakes, the quaint 1913 Kettle Falls Hotel offers lodging and meals.

Canoes and kayaks can be rented for paddling trips on the main lakes and also on the park's 26 smaller interior lakes, including those on the expansive Kabetogama Peninsula. Here, visitors can experience the peace and solitude of the North Woods wilderness, where loons "laugh" in nesting season and the howls of packs of gray wolves still enliven the nights. Black bears, white-tailed deer, and moose might also be encountered in the park's backcountry.

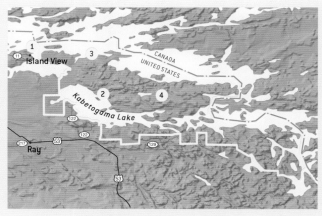

VOYAGEURS MINNESOTA

AREA
218,054 acres (882 sq km)

ESTABLISHED
April 1975

VISITOR INFORMATION
(218) 286 5258;
www.nps.gov/voya

KEY ATTRACTIONS ① Little American Island ② Ellsworth Rock Gardens ③ Rainy Lake Ice Road ④ Kabetogama Peninsula

NOTABLE WILDLIFE Gray wolf, black bear, moose, common loon, bald eagle

Bare granite shores surround many of the lakes within Voyageurs, in places revealing some of the oldest rocks on Earth. Although some trails can be reached by car, a boat is needed to explore all the park has to offer. Camping is popular on the remote lakes of the Kabetogama Peninsula.

Bald eagles are seen commonly in Voyageurs, nesting in tall trees along shorelines. Primarily fish-eaters, these magnificent raptors have made a comeback after serious populations decline traced to the pesticide DDT. The distinctive white head and tail are acquired when birds are three to five years old.

Glaciers scraped this landscape to bare rock in the most recent ice age, and in places vegetation covers underlying rock only thinly, or not at all. Some of the rock exposed on the surface here is among the oldest on Earth, composed of the early Precambrian granite of the Canadian Shield, as much as 2 billion years old.

In summer, park rangers lead several types of guided tours around the park, including trips to see historic sites such as the gold mines of Little American Island and to observe wildlife. The ranger-led North Canoe Voyage allows visitors to ride in an authentically styled 26-foot canoe similar to those used by the old-time *voyageurs*.

Though snow blankets the land in winter and the park's lakes freeze, visitation does not cease. Snowshoeing, cross-country skiing, and snowmobiling are popular seasonal activities, and the Rainy Lake Visitor Center remains open all year. A 7-mile-long ice road allows vehicles to travel across Rainy Lake to Cranberry Bay, offering a unique way to experience the park in winter.

THEODORE ROOSEVELT NATIONAL PARK

THEODORE ROOSEVELT, AMERICA'S greatest conservationist president, described the North Dakota Badlands best back in the late 19th century, when he wrote that parts of the terrain "are so fantastically broken in form and so bizarre in color as to seem hardly properly to belong to this Earth."

Yet the landscape does exist for all to see: deeply eroded bluffs striated in hues from gray to brown to yellow to red-orange; pillars, cones, and buttes in a multitude of forms; steep-sided ravines filled with junipers and cottonwoods; and through it all the Little Missouri River, a twisting ribbon of water in a parched land. Theodore Roosevelt National Park, one of the country's most under-appreciated parks, offers rugged scenery, fascinating wildlife, and rich history, all easily accessible along roads and trails.

The park took its name from the legendary outdoorsman who was the 26th president of the United States. Theodore Roosevelt first came to North Dakota as a 24-year-old in 1883, on a trip to hunt bison, and was greatly influenced by what he experienced. He acquired financial interest in two cattle ranches here, both of which he later sold when severe winters devastated the herds. Roosevelt saw massive bison herds decimated by overhunting, saw the land being abused, and he spent the rest of his life working for conservation of wildlife and other natural resources.

Today's park visitors can tour the Maltese Cross cabin, the small log building that was Theodore Roosevelt's first home in Dakota Territory.

Theodore Roosevelt National Park is made up of three separate units. The South Unit, located along Interstate 94, contains a scenic loop drive along with trails and other developments such as campgrounds and horseback riding; it is the park's most visited area. The North Unit, a 70-mile drive from the South Unit, offers campgrounds, trails, and a scenic drive. In between is the mostly undeveloped Elkhorn Ranch Unit, site of one of Roosevelt's ranches. Almost nothing remains of the ranch structures, and visitors should check with a ranger before attempting to reach the Elkhorn Ranch area.

The park's most popular attraction is the South Unit's 36-mile Scenic Loop Drive, which combines many of the park's best features along a paved road. Overlooks and interpretive signs provide insight into geology, flora, and fauna. The route passes veins of lignite coal, formed from plant material millions of years ago. In places, this coal has burned (often because of lightning strikes) and become a brick-like substance called scoria. The short Coal Vein Trail leads to a site where an underground seam of coal burned from 1951 to 1977, baking the adjacent sand and clay.

The Boicourt Overlook is one of several places on the drive offering spectacular views of Badlands terrain, a multicolored jumble of eroded hills and canyons that takes on even more striking hues at sunset. The short Wind Canyon Trail leads to a more pastoral vista, a view of the Little Missouri River and its cottonwood-shaded banks.

Much of the park's wildlife might be spotted from the Scenic Loop Drive. Bison (sometimes called buffalo) wander widely throughout the park. Their massive size and speed should be shown respect by remaining well away from them. Pronghorns graze in open areas, occasionally demonstrating their incredible

Caprocks of erosion-resistant material lie atop softer clay, creating columns that are among the diverse geological features of the Badlands. The varied terrain of the park can be viewed from overlooks along two scenic drives or explored on numerous trails, some of which lead deep into the backcountry.

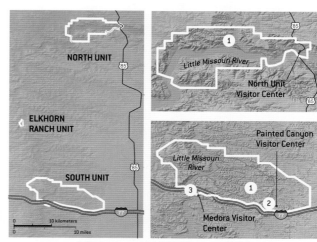

THEODORE ROOSEVELT NORTH DAKOTA

AREA
70,447 acres (285 sq km)
ESTABLISHED
November 1978
VISITOR INFORMATION
(701) 623 4466;
www.nps.gov/thro

KEY ATTRACTIONS ① Scenic drives ② Painted Canyon Overlook ③ Maltese Cross cabin
NOTABLE WILDLIFE Bison, elk, pronghorn, mule and white-tailed deer, black-tailed prairie dog, feral horse

The Little Missouri River forms a green ribbon as it winds through the North Dakota Badlands, its banks lined with cottonwoods and willows. "From the edges of the valley the land rises abruptly in steep high buttes whose crests are sharp and jagged," Theodore Roosevelt wrote of this bleak but beautiful landscape.

Feral horses roam Theodore Roosevelt National Park in herds of five to 15, each led by a dominant stallion. Some are believed to be descendants of horses that have lived freely in the Badlands since the 19th century, and resemble the horses in paintings of the "Wild West" by artists such as Frederic Remington and Charles M. Russell.

Several hundred bison live in Theodore Roosevelt National Park, reminders of the days when millions roamed the Great Plains in herds of awe-inspiring size. Males can weigh a ton and run at 35 miles per hour. Visitors should use caution around bison, which, though usually docile, can charge if provoked.

speed. Both mule deer and white-tailed deer reside in the park, as do elk, badgers, and porcupines. The park is home to several prairie-dog "towns," where these social rodents live in underground tunnels.

One of the most superb panoramas of the South Unit can be enjoyed from the Painted Canyon Visitor Center. The word "painted" indeed applies to the landscape here, where barren hills striped like a layer cake rise among green slopes dotted with junipers. Elk are often seen from this overlook, as are some of the park's feral horses, descendants of mustangs that escaped from Spanish explorers, Plains Indians, and early settlers over hundreds of years.

The park's North Unit is known for its 14-mile Scenic Drive, with a number of overlooks interpreting geology and natural history. Among the attractions are cannonball concretions, spheres of sedimentary minerals that formed underground and were exposed by erosion. One overlook

provides views of an area of bentonitic clay, bluish layers of very slippery rock, composed of volcanic ash, that causes small landslides when it gets wet.

The North Unit Scenic Drive ends at the Oxbow Overlook, with a view of a curving section of the Little Missouri River. Thousands of years ago, this stream flowed north, its waters eventually reaching Hudson Bay. During the most recent ice age, that route was blocked near this spot, and the Little Missouri cut a new course east to join the Missouri River.

The park maintains a herd of longhorn cattle in the North Unit, creating scenes like those that Theodore Roosevelt would have observed. North Unit hiking and horseback trails tend to be less used than those in the South Unit, and backcountry walkers often find the kind of solitude that the earliest settlers experienced, before ranches and farms spread across the Great Plains.

BADLANDS NATIONAL PARK

THE SIOUX INDIANS CALLED THE HEAVILY eroded terrain of the White River area *mako sica*, or "bad land." Some early European explorers dismissed the northern Great Plains as a worthless desert. But today, this land that was called "bad" for its rugged character and scarce water is highly valued for its spectacularly colorful scenery of pinnacles, buttes, crenelated cliffs, and cone-shaped hills.

Badlands National Park protects some of the best of this impressive landscape, including part of the Wall, a 60-mile-long cliff that separates the flatter prairie to the north from the bizarre world of the Badlands. One of the most amazing geological features of the upper Midwest, the Wall rises near vertically in places, is eroded into deep gullies in other areas, and is topped with an infinite variety of peaks, spires, and crests. Throughout the area, the varied formations show multicolored strata resulting from the rocks' differing origins as sediments of sand, silt, and clay, as well as layers of volcanic ash.

The park's Badlands Loop Road runs for 22 miles through the North Unit, from the Ben Reifel Visitor Center in the east to the Pinnacles Entrance in the north. Many of the park's major attractions are located along or near this route, including the Fossil Exhibit Trail, which tells the story of the rich deposit of fossils in the park. Paleontologists have excavated evidence of ancient horses, rhinoceroses, dogs, and birds, among other animals. Just north of the Ben Reifel Visitor Center, the half-mile loop Cliff Shelf Nature Trail climbs to a wonderful panorama of the White River Valley, and is an excellent spot for wildlife observation.

The Sage Creek Rim Road, in the northwestern part of the park, leads to a prairie dog town, and offers additional chances to see some of the park's diverse wildlife. Badlands National Park preserves one of the largest and most significant areas of

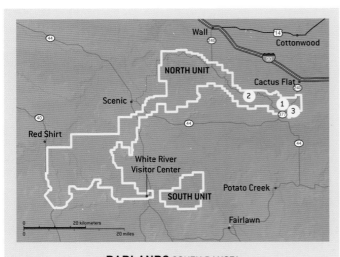

BADLANDS SOUTH DAKOTA

AREA
244,000 acres (987 sq km)

ESTABLISHED
November 1978

VISITOR INFORMATION
(605) 433 5361;
www.nps.gov/badl

KEY ATTRACTIONS ① The Wall
② Badlands Loop Road
③ Cliff Shelf Nature Trail

NOTABLE WILDLIFE Bison, bighorn sheep, pronghorn, swift fox, black-footed ferret

Deposition of material by ancient seas, rivers, and volcanoes built the Badlands over millions of years. Streams and rainfall erode the landscape in a relentless process that, if it continues at its present rate, will reduce the region to a flat plain in 500,000 years.

mixed-grass prairie (a transition zone between tallgrass prairie to the east and shortgrass prairie farther west) in North America, where bison, pronghorn, bighorn sheep, mule deer, and the rare swift fox roam. The endangered black-footed ferret has been reintroduced to the park, living in prairie dog towns.

In spring and early summer, especially after winters with abundant snow, the park's wildflower display can be breathtaking, with expanses of prairie dotted with coneflowers, sunflowers, evening primrose, Indian paintbrush, and dozens of other species.

Whether viewed from one of the many scenic overlooks along park roads or from a hiking trail through the 64,144 acres of backcountry wilderness, the fantastically sculpted rock formations of Badlands offer endless opportunity for exploration. Each vista changes throughout the day, varying from the long shadows and golden light of dawn and dusk to the blue skies and bright colors of midday.

The South Unit of Badlands National Park is managed in cooperation with the Oglala Lakota (Sioux) Nation. Little developed and offering few amenities, this area should be visited only after consultation with a park ranger. Information is available at the White River Visitor Center, which is staffed by members of the Oglala Lakota Nation.

A prairie dog gives an alarm cry to warn other members of its "town" of possible danger. These small rodents have been persecuted throughout their range in the American West and now exist in populations comprising less than 5 percent of their numbers before European settlement.

WIND CAVE NATIONAL PARK

DESIGNATED IN 1903 AS THE FIRST NATIONAL park anywhere on Earth established to protect a cave, Wind Cave offers visitors two very different but equally rewarding worlds to explore. Underground lies one of the world's longest caves, full of varied and beautiful speleothems (cave formations). On the surface, the park protects a large tract of mixed-grass prairie and ponderosa pine forest, as environmentally important as it is picturesque.

The Native Americans long knew of a "hole that breathes cool air" in the Black Hills region. Then, in 1881, two local brothers, Jesse and Tom Bingham, heard a whistling noise and found the cavern now known as Wind Cave. (The "wind" results from differing air pressure inside and outside the cave.) The exceptionally attractive formations discovered below ground led to a period of commercial tours, and later acquisition by the federal Department of the Interior.

Wind Cave is best known for an unusual and distinctive type of formation called boxwork, made of thin intersecting "fins" of calcite (crystallized calcium carbonate) resembling a giant honeycomb. Wind Cave is thought to have more of this odd and intricate formation than any other cave. In addition, the cave features formations such as cave popcorn (knobs of calcium carbonate), helictite bushes (clusters of curving or angular formations), frostwork (needle-like aragonite growths), and flowstones and draperies (sheetlike deposits of calcite), displayed in rooms with descriptive names including Eastern Star, Post Office, Devil's Lookout, Cathedral, and Fairgrounds.

A 19th-century explorer wrote that he had "given up the idea of finding the end of Wind Cave"—as it turned out, with good reason. Spelunkers have discovered more and more interconnected passages here, with the result that Wind Cave is

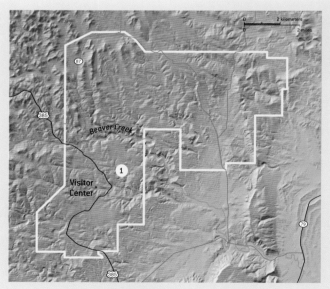

WIND CAVE SOUTH DAKOTA

AREA
28,295 acres (114 sq km)

ESTABLISHED
January 1903

VISITOR INFORMATION
(605) 745 4600;
www.nps.gov/wica

KEY ATTRACTIONS ① Wind Cave
NOTABLE WILDLIFE Bison, elk, pronghorn, mule and white-tailed deer, black-tailed prairie dog, wild turkey, sharp-tailed grouse

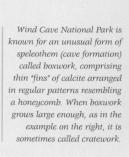

Wind Cave National Park is known for an unusual form of speleothem (cave formation) called boxwork, comprising thin "fins" of calcite arranged in regular patterns resembling a honeycomb. When boxwork grows large enough, as in the example on the right, it is sometimes called cratework.

Wind Cave National Park protects an important tract of mixed-grass prairie, a habitat found where the tallgrass prairie of the eastern Great Plains meets the shortgrass prairie found farther west. Bison, pronghorn, and prairie dogs make the prairie their home.

A small cavity or pocket inside a rock is referred to by geologists as a vug. These hollows have a variety of origins, and are often lined with different materials than those of their exteriors. This striking vug from Wind Cave is lined with crystals, giving it the appearance of some fierce creature's mouth.

Explorers make their way through Wind Cave's Snowdrift Avenue. This part of the cave was named for the extensive amount of frostwork of aragonite (a form of calcium carbonate) found on the walls. Over the years, cave explorers have discovered more than 130 miles of passages.

Boxwork is found in Wind Cave to an extent and in forms unknown in any other cave. Created when thin sheets of calcite intersect to form box-like shapes, boxwork exists primarily in the middle and lower levels of the cave. The fins may represent veins of calcite running through a matrix of limestone that has since eroded away.

now the world's fourth-longest cave system, stretching to more than 130 miles. Some of the remote passages can be seen on the Wild Cave Tour, in which participants crawl through tight passages wearing helmets, headlamps, and kneepads.

Above ground, Wind Cave National Park is home to herds of bison, elk, and pronghorn, as well as prairie dog towns typical of the mixed-grass environment of the Great Plains. Scenes from overlooks are reminiscent of those that greeted pioneers of the mid-19th century, with great numbers of animals grazing in expansive grassland, surrounded by low, rounded hills covered in ponderosa pine. Mule and white-tailed deer are seen often, and coyotes range the park, hunting cottontail rabbits and occasionally taking a young pronghorn.

Bison were reintroduced to Wind Cave in 1913, when the species was in the first stages of recovery after almost being wiped out by over-hunting and loss of habitat. The park's bison are known for being genetically pure, with no history of interbreeding with domestic cattle. Today, park visitors can enjoy the awe-inspiring sight of huge bull bison, which can be 6 feet high, and hear the roar given during the breeding season.

Saint Mary Lake, on the eastern side of Glacier National Park, reflects mountains carved into blade-like points by the massive glaciers of the most recent ice ages. Few places in North America provide such a landscape-scale textbook of glacial sculpting as does this expansive park in northwestern Montana.

GLACIER NATIONAL PARK

WITH ITS IMPOSING MOUNTAIN PEAKS, sheer cliffs, deep valleys, sky-blue alpine lakes, and meadows dotted with wildflowers, Glacier National Park possesses such an incredible bounty of scenery that its distinctive features seem crowded within its borders, despite its expansive area of 1,580 square miles. The Blackfeet Indians called this part of the northern Rocky Mountains the "backbone of the world," and the description seems apt for these bare summits following the Continental Divide through western Montana, reaching to the Canadian border.

Tourist development began here as early as the 19th century, when trains brought visitors who rode horses, walked, or took boats into the backcountry. Luckily for later generations, conservationists pushed for protection of the area, and Glacier was named America's 10th national park in 1910. A few hotels and chalets remain from those early days of tourism, but most of the park remains untouched by development. Glacier National Park has been designated both an International Biosphere Reserve and a World Heritage Site.

Contrary to popular interpretation, the park's name comes not so much from the glaciers found here today, but instead from the massive icefields of more than 10,000 years ago, whose actions shaped this spectacular landscape. Throughout the park are mountainsides carved into vertical cliffs, U-shaped valleys, bowl-like cirques, sharp-pointed mountaintop horns, and other physical features typical of a glacier-sculpted terrain. In 1850, there were an estimated 150 glaciers within the region that is now the national park. The current count is 26, and scientists

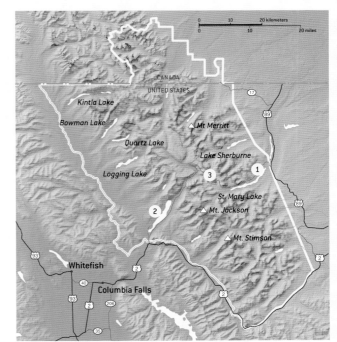

GLACIER MONTANA

AREA
1,013,322 acres (4,101 sq km)
ESTABLISHED
May 1910
VISITOR INFORMATION
(406) 888 7800;
www.nps.gov/glac

KEY ATTRACTIONS ① Going-to-the-Sun Road ② Lake McDonald ③ Garden Wall
NOTABLE WILDLIFE Grizzly bear, black bear, mountain goat, bighorn sheep, gray wolf, moose, lynx

High-elevation terrain near Logan Pass shows the rugged summits and sheer cliffs typical of the spectacular scenery in Glacier National Park. Going-to-the-Sun Highway provides motorists with a succession of breathtaking views along its 50-mile route across the park, including distant vistas of remaining glaciers.

Mountain goats are nearly as iconic to Glacier National Park as are grizzly bears, part of a diversity of animal species unparalleled in the lower 48 states. Of the large mammals living here when Europeans arrived on the scene, only the woodland caribou and bison are no longer present within the park.

Around 300 grizzly bears roam the national park, spending most of their time feeding on plant material, from roots to berries to pine nuts. Cubs learn from sow bears how to utilize different food sources during the course of the year. Hikers in the park should be aware of ways to minimize the risk of encounters with grizzlies.

warn that all of them may disappear by the year 2030 if current climate trends of warmer temperatures continue.

Much of the best of Glacier National Park's scenery can be enjoyed with relative ease thanks to the engineering marvel called Going-to-the-Sun Road. Winding through the park east–west for 50 miles, it was completed in 1932 and still amazes visitors in the way it snakes around mountainsides and along cliffs. In fact, the road has been named a National Historic Landmark. Topping out at 6,646 feet at Logan Pass, it allows those unable to hike a chance to see glaciers, wildlife, and the magical alpine world at and above the treeline, where vegetation is stunted by long winters and bitter winds.

In the southwestern part of the park, Going-to-the-Sun Road passes alongside Lake McDonald, the park's largest body of water. It then reaches surging McDonald Falls and ascends toward the Continental Divide and the famed Garden Wall, an imposing cliff rising vertically above forested ridges. At length the road reaches Jackson Glacier Overlook, where one of the park's remaining glaciers can be seen, and then winds south of Going-to-the-Sun Mountain, the peak that gave the road its name. The route then skirts Saint Mary Lake before reaching the park's eastern boundary. Saint Mary Lake is one of several places within the park where guided boat tours are offered to see scenery and wildlife. Trailheads around the lake lead to the impressive Saint Mary Falls and Virginia Falls.

Two developed areas are reached by dead-end roads leading into the eastern part of the park. The Many Glacier and Two Medicine areas both feature ranger stations, camping, boat tours, and multiple hiking trails. The 1914 Many Glacier Hotel, still in operation, is listed on the National Register of Historic Places. Of the many trails here, one popular route takes a close look at Grinnell Glacier, one of the largest icefields in the park.

Visitors traveling the length of Going-to-the-Sun Road will notice that the environments of Glacier National Park change from the west side of the Continental Divide to the east. The western slopes receive more rainfall, and are cloaked with lush coniferous forests of western red cedar, hemlock, spruce, and fir. The eastern side of the park, in the rain shadow of the Rocky Mountains, receives less moisture, and features grasslands with scattered groves of aspen and limber pine.

The park's range of elevation and varied habitats make it home to a dazzling array of wildlife. Most famous is the grizzly bear, which exists here in one of the largest remaining populations in the lower 48 states. Other large mammals include mountain goats, elk, bighorn sheep, gray wolves, moose, and mountain lions. Birdwatchers know Glacier as a place to look for such sought-after species as the beautiful harlequin duck, the aquatic dipper, the rare and elusive black swift, and the white-tailed ptarmigan, resident above the treeline.

Among the most dramatic and famous sights in America's national parks, the Grand Canyon of the Yellowstone has the power to awe all those who stand at its edge and look toward 308-foot-high Lower Falls. Paintings of the canyon by 19th-century artist Thomas Moran helped convince Congress to create Yellowstone National Park.

YELLOWSTONE NATIONAL PARK

IN THE MID-19TH CENTURY, TRAVELERS began to report on a fantastic place in the American West where geysers shot scalding water high into the air, mudholes bubbled like boiling soup, and steam escaped from countless holes in the Earth. At a time when wildlife was being destroyed by the advance of settlement across the West, this place was still a paradise for animals. Amid tall mountain peaks, waterfalls thundered down spectacular canyons.

As a result, the United States declared Yellowstone as the country's—and the world's—first national park in 1872, creating a new concept in the relationship between people and nature. Established long before the creation of the National Park Service, Yellowstone was for its early decades protected by cavalry units of the U.S. Army.

It is fitting that Yellowstone National Park holds such an important place in the history of the conservation movement. Few, if any, other parks combine such awe-inspiring scenery, dazzling geology, diverse and abundant wildlife, and intriguing history. Yellowstone boasts more than 10,000 geothermal features, including more than 300 geysers—nearly two-thirds of the world's geysers. Other features include mudpots, fumaroles (steam vents), and hot springs in a rainbow of colors.

Around 600,000 years ago, a massive volcanic explosion occurred here, leaving a caldera (collapsed crater) of more than 1,300 square miles. Subsequent lava flows covered part of the area, which was then buried under glaciers in the most recent ice age. Yellowstone's modern landscape reflects all these events and more, including mountain-building and erosion of deep canyons.

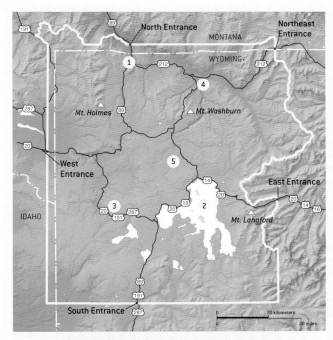

YELLOWSTONE WYOMING, MONTANA, IDAHO

AREA
2,219,790 acres (8,983 sq km)

ESTABLISHED
March 1872

VISITOR INFORMATION
(307) 344 7381;
www.nps.gov/yell

KEY ATTRACTIONS ① Mammoth Hot Springs ② Yellowstone Lake ③ Old Faithful ④ Tower Falls ⑤ Hayden Valley

NOTABLE WILDLIFE Grizzly bear, black bear, elk, bison, gray wolf, bighorn sheep, pronghorn, moose

One of the most popular sites in Upper Geyser Basin, Morning Glory Pool shows colors created by heat-tolerant bacteria. Unfortunately, its vivid colors have faded over the years as visitors have thrown coins and rocks into the pool, causing its temperature to decrease and making the blue center less vivid.

The striking terraces of Mammoth Hot Springs are formed of travertine, a mineral created by water flowing through limestone. The exact location of springs changes continuously, resulting in constant alterations in the size and appearance of the terraces.

Many of the park's most famous features are found within the Upper, Lower, and Midway Geyser Basins, in the southwestern part of Yellowstone. The Upper Geyser Basin is home to Old Faithful, the world's most famous geyser, which erupts about 20 times daily, shooting water as high as 180 feet into the air for up to five minutes. The line-up of fabulous geothermal features in Lower Geyser Basin includes Great Fountain Geyser, a superb display of gushing water (though it erupts only twice a day), and multicolored Fountain Paint Pots. In Midway Geyser Basin, visitors can marvel at Grand Prismatic Spring, Yellowstone's largest hot spring, 370 feet in diameter and named for the gorgeous prismatic-type colors it displays. The main park road leads north past other sights such as Artist Paint Pots, displaying the colors of an artist's palette, and Firehole Canyon Drive, a side road leading along the Firehole River and the whitewater of Firehole Falls.

The Mammoth Hot Springs area, in northwestern Yellowstone, is named for the amazing springs where hot water deposits limestone as a striking series of terraces. Here, too, are the historically significant buildings of Fort Yellowstone, constructed beginning in 1891 for the soldiers who were assigned to protect park wildlife and other resources. The park entrance road north of Mammoth is a good place to look for pronghorn, in the grassy flats, and bighorn sheep, on the rocks above the highway.

In the central area of Yellowstone are found the park's most spectacular vistas, centering on the Grand Canyon of the Yellowstone. Twenty miles long, this awesome chasm, carved by the Yellowstone River, can be viewed from many lookout points. Its major features are the impressive Upper Falls, which are 109 feet high, and the Lower Falls, at 308 feet high. The canyon walls, tinted in hues ranging from red to yellow by heat and chemical reactions, gave the park its name. At the northern end of the canyon area, Tower Falls drops 132 feet amid a striking setting of eroded volcanic spires.

To the south of the Grand Canyon of the Yellowstone, Hayden Valley holds near legendary status as a place to enjoy the park's wildlife. Bison and elk are often seen here in substantial herds, and in spring, when their young are born, grizzly bears arrive to prey on the vulnerable newborn animals. Bald eagles soar above the valley, where sandhill cranes and white pelicans nest. Here, the Yellowstone River flows placidly in broad curves, providing nesting areas for waterfowl.

In the center of the park, Yellowstone Lake ranks as the largest high-altitude lake in North America. Beneath its surface, scientists have discovered an array of steam vents, hot springs, and other geothermal features. Many mudpots, hot springs, and other features are also found on the surface in the Yellowstone Lake area, and new ones appear regularly. Some can be seen from park trails, while others areas may be visited only on ranger-led tours because of the dangerous conditions around them. Also near the lake is the trail to Natural Bridge, a 51-foot-high arch eroded from rhyolite, one of the many types of volcanic rock in the park. Moose are sometimes seen in the Yellowstone Lake area.

Overlooked by some park visitors, the Lamar Valley in the northeastern part of Yellowstone National Park is also a superb location for wildlife watching. Drier and more open than most other areas in the park, it is a good place to spot pronghorn, the speedy mammal often called antelope, although it is not a member of the true antelope family. Lamar Valley is also a likely place to see gray wolves, which roam the park in a dozen or more packs.

Winter brings harsh conditions to Yellowstone National Park, but wildlife species find ways to survive. This bison, for example, warms itself in a steam vent. Most park roads close in winter, but visitors can explore the park on guided snowcoach, snowmobile, snowshoe, and bus tours.

GRAND TETON NATIONAL PARK

AMERICAN'S NATIONAL PARKS ABOUND IN fabulous scenery, but no park surpasses Grand Teton in the sheer beauty of its landscape: its rugged mountain peaks rising above mirror-like lakes, its expansive valley bordered by forests, with the Snake River meandering in broad curves. Stark granite summits, dense coniferous forests, rushing streams, wildflower-bright meadows—all these and more compose the world of Grand Teton. The park lies just south of Yellowstone National Park, separated by the John D. Rockefeller Jr. Memorial Parkway.

The stunning panoramas that greet park visitors were born in geological events dating back millions of years. Beaneath the ground here is a great break in the Earth's crust called the Teton Fault, running north–south for 40 miles. Around 10 million years ago, the area on the west began to rise, while the area on the east began to sink. The two sections have since moved as much as 30,000 feet in relation to each other. This displacement resulted in one of the most distinctive features of the Grand Teton terrain: the abrupt rise of mountains from the adjacent lowlands, with few foothills between. In a relatively short distance within the national park, elevations range from 6,400 feet on the valley floor to 13,770 feet at the peak of the mountain called the Grand Teton.

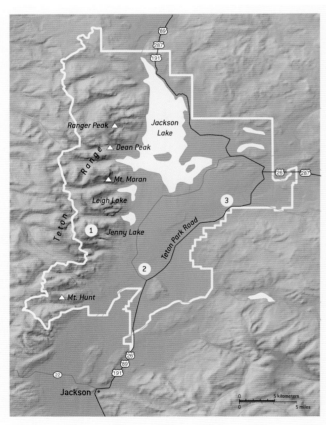

GRAND TETON WYOMING

AREA
309,995 acres (1,255 sq km)

ESTABLISHED
February 1929

VISITOR INFORMATION
(307) 739 3300;
www.nps.gov/grte

KEY ATTRACTIONS ① Grand Teton ② Jackson Hole ③ Snake River

NOTABLE WILDLIFE Bison, elk, moose, pronghorn, grizzly and black bears, mule deer, bald and golden eagles

Boaters on the Snake River enjoy a view of 12,605-foot Mount Moran, with the golden fall foliage of aspen trees adding color to the scene. One of the most impressive peaks in Grand Teton National Park, Mount Moran hosts Skillet Glacier on its east face, one of a dozen park glaciers fed by around 15 feet of snow each winter.

Much more recently (in geological time), periods of glaciation have shaped the landscape, creating steep cliffs, knife-edge ridges, U-shaped valleys, mountain lakes, and other glacial features. All this activity—tectonic movement with occasional massive earthquakes, sculpting by vast sheets of ice, erosion by water and wind—has created a meeting point of mountains and plains that is especially imposing, with scenery of visual immediacy as well as beauty.

The centerpiece of Grand Teton National Park is an array of the tallest mountains in the Teton Range that has come to be called the Cathedral Group, in recognition of the grandeur of its awesome summits. The Grand Teton dominates the skyline, flanked by South Teton, Middle Teton, Mount Owen, and Teewinot Mountain. The glacier-shaped form of many of the range's peaks inspired early French explorers to give them the name "*tetons*," or breasts. A few glaciers remain on the mountain slopes, which receive an average of 15 feet of snow each winter.

Wildlife of the Teton Range includes grizzly and black bears, mountain lions, bighorn sheep, yellow-bellied marmots, and the small rabbit-like animals called pikas. The hike up Cascade Canyon, just north of Mount Owen and Teewinot Mountain, offers a good chance to see Grand Teton fauna, as well as the 200-foot cascade called Hidden Falls.

Just to the east of the Teton Range lie several beautiful lakes, including Phelps, Jenny, Leigh, and Jackson (by far the largest), as well as many smaller lakes and ponds. Hiking trails lead to and around some of the lakes, which on calm mornings offer stunning reflective views of the great mountains towering above them.

Mountain men of the 19th century gave the name "holes" to mountain-ringed valleys of the American West. The broad valley east of the Tetons, called Jackson Hole, is covered in grasses and sagebrush, and is home to a notable diversity of wildlife. Bison, elk, and mule deer are often seen grazing in the valley, which also hosts herds of pronghorn in summer. Able to reach speeds of 70 miles per hour, pronghorn are the fastest land animals in the western hemisphere. Coyotes are commonly seen trotting across Jackson Hole, on the lookout for ground squirrels, young pronghorn or mule deer, and other prey.

The Snake River, which begins north of the park and flows into Jackson Lake, exits that body of water to wind through the floor of Jackson Hole, its tree-lined banks providing additional habitat for a variety of wildlife. Moose are sometimes seen grazing on riverside willows. Canada geese, sandhill cranes, various ducks, bald eagles, and ospreys are among the birds that frequent the Snake. Rafting, canoeing, and kayaking are popular on the river both above and below Jackson Lake. Placid sections of the Snake River offer safe boating for beginners, while whitewater segments challenge experienced paddlers.

When Grand Teton National Park was established in 1929, it comprised only the Teton Range and the adjacent lakes. Jackson Hole and the Snake River were added to park boundaries in 1950 in recognition of their beauty and value as wildlife habitat.

The park's highest peak, 13,770-foot Grand Teton, rises above the valley of Jackson Hole. Flanked by Middle Teton and Mount Owen, Grand Teton is the centerpiece of the group of mountains called the Cathedral Group. The picturesque barn is part of the collection of historic buildings called Mormon Row.

The national park is bordered on the south by the National Elk Refuge, home to more than 5,000 elk—the world's largest wintering concentration of these elegant mammals. In winter, a concession firm offers horse-drawn sleigh rides to view the herds. In summer, bison and bighorn sheep can be seen on the refuge.

Moose are most often seen in wetland areas of the park, especially sites with willows—one of their favorite foods. Ponds created where beaver have dammed a stream are good locations to spot these large members of the deer family. Males expend a significant amount of energy to grow their huge antlers each year.

While many areas of the park are accessible only to hikers and backpackers, much can be enjoyed from park roads and the overlooks located along them. U.S. Highway 191 runs the length of the park and offers many fine viewpoints of the Cathedral Group and the Snake River. Teton Park Road traverses the center of the park, providing access to such popular locations as Menors Ferry Historic District (where an early settler set up a ferry service across the Snake River in 1894) and Jenny Lake.

Some of the best roadside views in the park can be reached on the Jenny Lake Scenic Drive, a turning off Teton Park Road. This route also provides access to the trailheads for hikes around String and Leigh Lakes, stunning bodies of water that rank among the park's most popular destinations. Farther north off Teton Park Road, a dead-end side road winds to the top of 7,953-foot Signal Mountain. Though not among the park's highest peaks, Signal Mountain, because of its location, offers one of the best panoramic vistas of Jackson Hole and Lake Jackson, with the Teton Range looming to the west.

The warm summer season is brief in Grand Teton National Park, but the arrival of cold weather does not bring an end to park activities. In the fall, rangers lead wildlife-viewing trips, and elk give their "bugling" mating calls. In winter, the park offers guided snowshoeing walks. Though most roads are closed and daily high temperatures from December to February average below freezing, the blanket of snow that covers Grand Teton adds another element to its incomparable beauty.

ROCKY MOUNTAIN NATIONAL PARK

IN A STATE KNOWN FOR ITS SPECTACULAR mountains—there are more than 50 peaks over 14,000 feet in Colorado—Rocky Mountain National Park stands out for its beauty, wildlife, and recreational opportunities. With lush wetlands, vast tracts of coniferous forest, dozens of pristine mountain lakes, and extensive areas of alpine environment above the treeline, the park fully deserves its ranking among America's most popular national parks.

The Continental Divide winds through Rocky Mountain National Park, which encompasses more than 60 summits over 12,000 feet within its 415 square miles. The park's high point is 14,259-foot Longs Peak. Because of the rain-shadow effect of weather patterns moving west to east, the western side of the park receives significantly more annual precipitation than does the eastern part. In the west are broad, marshy meadows bordering the upper reaches of the Colorado River, while much of the east comprises drier foothills of open ponderosa pine forest. Scattered throughout are the flat inter-mountain valleys that Colorado residents call "parks," such as the popular camping and picnicking area called Moraine Park, near the national park's eastern entrance.

Much of the landscape within Rocky Mountain National Park is the legacy of the most recent ice ages. Glaciers moved down valleys, leaving behind the classic U-shaped terrain indicative of their action, as well as large moraines: ridges of rock pushed aside as glaciers slowly moved downward. Some small glaciers still endure within the park, high up on alpine slopes. They are often found within cirques, or glacier-carved bowls seen on mountainsides.

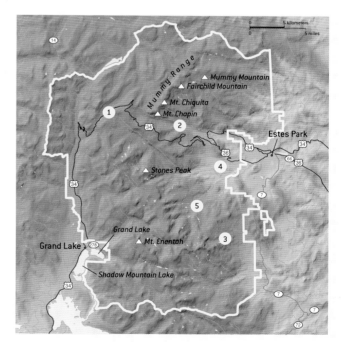

ROCKY MOUNTAIN COLORADO

AREA
265,758 acres (1,075 sq km)
ESTABLISHED
January 1915
VISITOR INFORMATION
(970) 586 1206;
www.nps.gov/romo

KEY ATTRACTIONS ① Trail Ridge Road ② Old Fall River Road ③ Longs Peak ④ Moraine Park ⑤ Bear Lake
NOTABLE WILDLIFE Bighorn sheep, elk, black bear, moose, mule deer, mountain lion

With its distinctive notched top and sheer east face, 14,259-foot Longs Peak is the highest point in the national park. Around one-third of the 265,000-acre park is composed of alpine tundra, the environment above the treeline where plants and animals have adapted to survive harsh winter conditions.

Famed for their glorious golden fall foliage, aspens grow in clusters in which all trees are clones, connected by a common root system. Flattened petioles (leaf stems) cause leaves to quiver in the slightest breeze, giving this species the common name "quaking aspen." The smooth white bark develops dark patches with age.

Low-lying parts of the park, including riparian areas along streams, are home to trees and shrubs such as willow, alder, quaking aspen, and birch, browsed by mule deer, elk, and moose. Ponderosa pine and juniper grow on adjoining slopes, blending higher into forests dominated by subalpine fir, Engelmann spruce, and limber pine. Mountain lions, black bears, and snowshoe hares are among the mammal species frequenting the middle elevations of the park.

At an elevation of around 11,200 feet, climatic conditions become too harsh for tree growth, and the few individual trees surviving at the treeline often show stunted, twisted shapes. Above the treeline grow only small, low-profile plants that can exist in an environment where snow covers the ground as much as eight months of the year. Grasses, sedges, cushion plants, and lichens make up much of the alpine plant life; wildflowers must bloom quickly to take advantage of brief summer sunshine. Bighorn sheep live part of the year in this starkly beautiful landscape, browsing amid the rock outcrops. The white-tailed ptarmigan is the best-known bird resident here, changing its plumage from summer brown to winter white for camouflage.

Rocky Mountain National Park is home to Trail Ridge Road, the highest continuous paved road in the national park system, and unquestionably one of the most scenic drives on the planet. Beginning in lush valleys dotted with beaver ponds, the route ascends steeply along mountainsides and through forests of spruce and fir. Overlooks provide breathtaking views of mountain summits, deep valleys, and alpine lakes. Rising to an altitude of 12,183 feet, the road travels above the treeline for 11 miles, but people with heart problems or breathing difficulties are cautioned about traveling this highway because of the low oxygen content of the air. The Alpine Visitor Center, located at Fall River Pass, offers exhibits and programs on the park's alpine environment. Trail Ridge Road and the Alpine Visitor Center are open from about late May until mid-October, depending on weather conditions.

Another renowned drive, Bear Lake Road is one of the few paved roads on the continent leading to a true alpine lake environment. This route also provides access to trailheads for many of the park's most popular hiking routes, such as those to Loch Vale, Dream Lake, and Alberta Falls.

With more than 350 miles of trails, Rocky Mountain National Park offers nearly unlimited opportunities for hiking. Trails on the east side of the park are generally the most popular, but even here there are chances for solitary enjoyment of the wilderness, especially for those who start their hikes at dawn. An early start is mandatory for those who want to challenge Longs Peak, a very strenuous 16-mile round-trip that takes most hikers about 12 hours. Because of the possibility of afternoon summer storms with lightning, many Longs Peak hikers begin their ascent shortly after midnight. The trail to the summit is usually free of snow and ice only between mid-July and mid-September.

Horseback riding has long been a popular way to experience the beauty of the park. Two concessioner-operated stables are located within the park, and several others outside the park offer trail rides of various lengths. Guided rides offer even the inexperienced an opportunity to see off-road areas.

It is wise to be cautious about certain activities in Rocky Mountain. The high elevation means that visitors from lower areas may tire quickly until acclimatized; dehydration is common, and intense sunlight means a hat and sunscreen are mandatory. This is mountain lion country. While the chances of a dangerous encounter are slim, hikers should be aware of what to do if they meet a big cat on the trail, and parents should keep small children in sight at all times.

Almost driven to local extinction by overhunting and disease in the mid-20th century, bighorn sheep have made a partial recovery and now number several hundred in the park. Spending much of their time on sheer cliffs, bighorn can be observed visiting mineral licks in Horseshoe Park in late spring and summer.

Pads of water lilies dot the surface of Nymph Lake, just a short hike from the popular Bear Lake trailhead. The rugged profile of Hallett Peak in the distance shows the sculpting effect of glacial action. A least six major periods of glaciation have shaped park features over the past 700,000 years.

BLACK CANYON OF THE GUNNISON NATIONAL PARK

AMONG THE MOST AWE-INSPIRING geological features in North America, the Black Canyon of the Gunnison presents a dizzying sight to visitors who peer into its depths from one of the many overlooks along its rim. No other gorge on the continent combines such depth, narrowness, and verticality, giving the impression of a gigantic fissure opening straight down into the surface of the Earth.

Figures tell part of the story: the canyon drops more than a half-mile at its deepest, and in places is only 40 feet wide at the bottom. But numbers cannot convey the vision of the sheer walls, the infinitely varied rock outcrops and spires, and at the base, the rushing river that carved all this.

The Gunnison River became set in its course 10 to 15 million years ago as still-mysterious geological forces raised the surrounding Colorado Plateau. The stream cut down into relatively soft rock until it met harder Precambrian rock, almost 2 billion years old. Trapped in its course by the canyon it had already dug, unable to detour around the hard rock, it cut into the resistant material at the rate of about 1 inch every century. Over the past 2 million years, the river created the deep, steep-sided Black Canyon of the Gunnison.

Many of the best vistas in the park are easily accessible along the paved, 7-mile South Rim Drive, which features 12 overlooks. The main park visitor center is located near Gunnison Point, a superb overlook at a spot where the canyon is about 1,800 feet deep. Nearby nature trails provide an introduction to the ecology of the canyon rim area, where prominent plants include sagebrush, Gambel oak, pinyon pine, and juniper.

No officially maintained trails lead down to the bottom of the canyon from the South Rim Drive area. Such a trek is extremely strenuous and should be attempted only by fit and well-prepared hikers who have consulted with park rangers about the difficulties involved.

Among the most famous overlooks along the drive is the Painted Wall View, named for the striking 2,250-foot-high wall that is the highest cliff in Colorado. "Painted" refers to the huge veins of pinkish pegmatite, a variety of granite, that run through the wall like marbling in a piece of meat. The terminus of the dead-end drive is 8,289-foot High Point, the highest elevation in the park. A nature trail here leads to a view of the canyon at its deepest, some 2,700 feet from rim to river.

On the opposite side of the canyon, the gravel North Rim Drive offers the best views of the sheer cliffs and narrowest parts of the Inner Canyon. No bridge crosses the canyon in the park, so to travel from the

South Rim, where most facilities are located, to the North Rim requires a drive of 2 to 3 hours.

Incredible as it may seem, a narrow-gauge railroad was constructed in the 1880s through 15 miles of the Black Canyon, continuing service until 1949. One passenger was author Rudyard Kipling, who later wrote, "There was a glory and a wonder and a mystery about the mad ride." A mad ride also awaits kayakers and rafters who take up the challenge of the Gunnison River's Class V whitewater rapids, crashing and churning along the rocky course at the canyon's bottom.

Black Canyon of the Gunnison National Park encompasses 15 miles of the canyon's total length of 53 miles. The remainder of the gorge lies within Curecanti National Recreation Area, to the east of the national park, and Gunnison Gorge National Conservation Area, to the west.

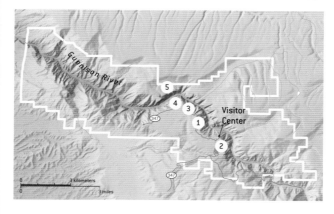

BLACK CANYON OF THE GUNNISON COLORADO

AREA
30,750 acres (124 sq km)

ESTABLISHED
October 1999

VISITOR INFORMATION
(970) 641 2337;
www.nps.gov/blca

KEY ATTRACTIONS ① Black Canyon ② Gunnison Point ③ Chasm View ④ Painted Wall ⑤ Exclamation Point

NOTABLE WILDLIFE Mule deer, bighorn sheep, elk, peregrine falcon, golden eagle

Slowly cutting downward over millions of years, the Gunnison River carved the Black Canyon as it eroded through sedimentary material of the Colorado Plateau and harder underlying rocks. Varied park habitats include forests of pine, oak, and juniper on the canyon rim and riparian hardwoods along the river.

The appealing American dipper spends its life along rocky, rushing streams, diving and swimming for aquatic insects and even nesting beside the water. This gray, stub-tailed bird was named for its constant characteristic bobbing or "dipping" motion as it walks or perches on rocks in rivers.

GREAT SAND DUNES NATIONAL PARK AND PRESERVE

COVERING MORE THAN 30 SQUARE MILES of a valley once filled by a huge ancient lake, the Great Sand Dunes of southern Colorado present a landscape unlike any other in North America, an otherworldly terrain resulting from a unique set of geological forces. In addition to the dunes themselves—a virtual sea of sand—the national park encompasses peaks of the Sangre de Cristo Range of the Rocky Mountains, a place of gorgeous alpine lakes and high-elevation wildlife.

These are the tallest dunes on the continent, with the highest, Star Dune, rising 750 feet from base to summit. The dunes' creation began with Lake Alamosa, which filled the valley between the San Luis Mountains and the Sangre de Cristo Range more than 3 million years ago. About 440,000 years ago, the lake broke through its southern bank and drained down the Rio Grande Valley. Lake Alamosa and later, now disappeared,

Winds constantly reshape the Great Sand Dunes, creating contours that are especially distinct with the low-angle sunlight of dawn and dusk. Early-morning hikers may find animal tracks in the sand, evidence of nocturnal visitors—though few animals venture far from the edges of the dune field.

smaller lakes left behind a massive quantity of sand. The opposing forces of prevailing westerly winds and storms blowing from the east push the sand upward, resulting in stupendously high dunes. In addition, creeks carry sand from the eastern part of the dunes to the south and west, where it is continuously "recycled" rather than being blown out of the valley. Historical photographs have shown that the Great Sand Dunes have remained relatively unchanged in their appearance for more than a century.

Visitors are free to hike across the vast dune field, climbing these mini-mountains to their summits for incredible panoramas of dunes stretching miles, with snow-covered peaks forming the horizon. Many people enjoy camping amid the dunes, enjoying evenings of solitude and quiet. The stars and planets of the night sky shine brilliantly here, undimmed by the light pollution of civilization. Others use sleds or snowboards to slide down dunes, "surfing" these mighty walls of sand.

Located on the eastern edge of the dunes, Medano Creek can be a rushing stream or bone dry, depending on winter snowfall and other precipitation. The creek sometimes exhibits an unusual condition called surge flow, when a temporary sand "dam" upstream gives way and sends a series of waves downstream.

The beautiful high country of the Sangre de Cristos offers an environment far different from the stark, barren dunes. Primitive roads and hiking trails climb through many different life zones: pinyon pines and junipers at low elevation give way to ponderosa pine and Douglas-fir, as well as aspen, which turns a brilliant yellow-gold in autumn. Still higher grow forests of spruce and fir, with treeless tundra covering the tops of mountains, some of which reach more than 13,000 feet and are snow-covered for nine months of the year.

From dune treks to long-distance hiking trips across the alpine world of the Rockies, Grand Sand Dunes National Park and Preserve offers visitors an array of experiences as wide as its landscape is diverse.

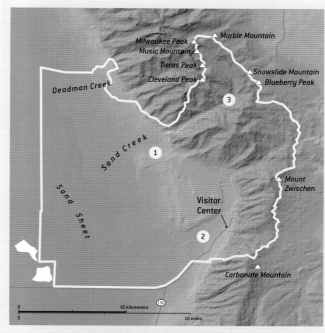

GREAT SAND DUNES COLORADO

AREA
149,138 acres (604 sq km)

ESTABLISHED
September 2004

VISITOR INFORMATION
(719) 378 6300;
www.nps.gov/grsa

KEY ATTRACTIONS ① Star Dune
② Medano Creek ③ Sangre de Cristo Range

NOTABLE WILDLIFE Elk, pronghorn, black bear, bighorn sheep, mountain lion

Offering a striking contrast to the barren dunes, the Sangre de Cristo Mountains rise to the east of the national park, reaching heights of more than 13,000 feet. Elk and bighorn sheep roam the slopes of these alpine peaks, which at their summits rise above the treeline to elevations where only low-lying plants such as grasses and mosses grow.

The largest cliff dwelling in Mesa Verde National Park, Cliff Palace is believed to have comprised 150 rooms and 23 kivas, or round, underground ceremonial structures. Archeologists say around 100 people occupied the site. Ancestral Puebloan people lived in the Mesa Verde area for 700 years.

MESA VERDE NATIONAL PARK

ON THE EDGE OF A BROAD, FLATTISH mesa in southwestern Colorado lies one of the most fascinating and mysterious sites within the National Park Service. Here, where the Colorado Plateau has been eroded into deep canyons and steep bluffs, visitors can explore extensive cliff dwellings and other structures built by people of the Ancestral Puebloan culture during the period from 1,400 to 700 years ago. The Ancestral Puebloans constructed spectacular masonry homes and ceremonial sites, some with scores of rooms, only to abandon them in a relatively short time for reasons that remain unknown.

Local ranchers of the 1880s were the first European-Americans known to have seen these ruins, which soon attracted the attention of archeologists. In 1906, President Theodore Roosevelt signed legislation establishing Mesa Verde National Park to "preserve the works of man," making this the first national park created for its archeological value, rather than its natural-history importance.

Despite centuries of erosion and a period when looters damaged the site, Mesa Verde endures as a haunting evocation of a once thriving community. Multi-storied buildings of native sandstone and round ceremonial chambers called kivas are the most notable of Mesa Verde's structures, which also comprise pit houses, towers, agricultural sites, and others related to daily community life. Taken all together, Mesa Verde protects some of the most important and best-preserved archeological ruins in the United States.

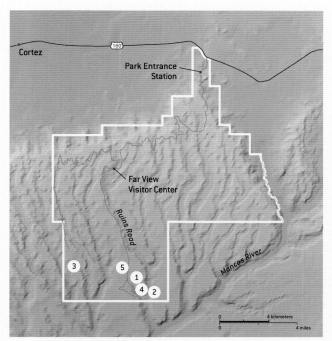

MESA VERDE COLORADO

AREA	**KEY ATTRACTIONS** ① Cliff Palace
52,485 acres (212 sq km)	② Balcony House ③ Long House
ESTABLISHED	④ Sun Temple ⑤ Chapin Mesa
June 1906	Archeological Museum
VISITOR INFORMATION	**NOTABLE WILDLIFE** Elk, mule deer,
(970) 529 4465;	black bear, mountain lion, wild
www.nps.gov/meve	turkey, peregrine falcon

Visitors should plan trips to Mesa Verde between mid-April and mid-October, when all park visitor centers and other facilities are open. The adventure begins along the long, winding entrance road, which traverses woodland of juniper, pine, and Douglas-fir. The road passes several splendid lookout points, with views of the cliffs and canyons of the mesa. A side route off the main entrance road leads to the overlook at 8,427-foot Park Point, the highest elevation in the park, with a breathtaking panoramic view of surrounding terrain. Horizontal strata exposed on bluffs, in shades of tan and yellow, reflect the origin of park sandstone as sedimentary layers in ancient seas and coastal swamps.

A stop at the Far View Visitor Center is mandatory to experience three of the most notable structures within the park: Cliff Palace, Balcony House, and Long House, all of which can be seen only on ranger-guided tours for which tickets are required. Some cliff dwellings, such as Spruce Tree House, and other park sites may be seen on ranger-led or self-guided tours, depending on the site and the season.

Several of Mesa Verde's finest structures are found in the Chapin Mesa area, in the extreme southern part of the park. This area is also home to the Chapin Mesa Archeological Museum, which provides an introduction to Ancestral Puebloan culture. Although the Mesa Verde area was occupied for around 700 years, it was only during the last century of its habitation that the famed cliff dwellings were constructed. Before that time, its people lived in pit houses (shallow excavations roofed with timbers) and adobe and masonry houses on the top of the mesa.

Nearby Spruce Tree House is the third largest of the cliff dwellings at Mesa Verde, and demonstrates the way the Ancestral Puebloans used large natural alcoves in the sandstone bluffs to build their homes and kivas during the last century they lived here. With the remains of about 130 rooms and eight kivas, Spruce Tree House has been remarkably well preserved by the overhanging cliff under which it sits. Its rock walls pierced by doors and windows, its great variety of rooms, its circular kivas—all give tantalizing hints of what life must have been like for a thriving community of hundreds of residents.

Also in the Chapin Mesa area are Cliff Palace, the largest cliff dwelling at Mesa Verde, with 150 rooms including 21 kivas; and Balcony House, a 40-room cliff dwelling. Tours to both these sites require visitors to negotiate stairs and ladders and are regarded as somewhat strenuous.

The Wetherill Mesa area, in the western part of the park, is home to Long House, the second largest cliff dwelling in the park. Reached by a tram from the parking area, Long House is tucked into a massive rock arch, a setting of striking beauty. No one knows why the Ancestral Puebloans began building their dwelling under cliffs after centuries of living atop the mesa. The reasons could have involved protection from weather, defense against enemies, or some still undiscovered motivation.

Mesa Verde National Park preserves more than 4,700 archeological sites, with only a small percentage of them the large cliff dwellings that have come to symbolize the park. The great majority of cliff dwellings contain ten or fewer rooms, and there are thousands of other Ancestral

Point Lookout, a distinctive geological feature along the Mesa Verde entrance road, is composed of sandstone that began as beaches and sand bars along an ancient ocean shore. The relatively durable sandstone protects underlying softer rock from erosion. A trail leads to the 8,571-foot top of the mesa.

Mule deer are common at Mesa Verde National Park, preyed upon by mountain lions and bobcats. The fawns, unable to run as fast as adults can, are especially vulnerable. Their pattern of spots provides camouflage, mimicking the look of dappled sunlight and shade as they hide in forest or under shrubs.

Ancestral Puebloans built the structures at Mesa Verde with sandstone, mortar, and wooden beams. Sandstone was shaped into rough blocks using hard river stones, then fixed in place with mortar made of soil, ash, and water. Decorative plasterwork that covered some walls has been lost to erosion.

Puebloan sites associated with their life of hunting and farming beans, corn, and squash, as well as their religious and ceremonial activities.

One example is Cedar Tree Tower, located off the Chapin Mesa Road, a stone tower and associated kiva that may have been used for religious purposes, astronomical observations or communication. Sun Temple, located south of the Chapin Mesa Archeological Museum, is a large D-shaped structure that is believed to have been used for ceremonial purposes. Its massive walls may once have

stood 14 feet high. Elsewhere in the park are the remains of dams used to store water for irrigation, petroglyphs, and terraces for the efficient planting of crops.

Although the Ancestral Puebloans are sometimes referred to as a "vanished" people, they did not in fact disappear when they left Mesa Verde around 1300 c.e. Their descendants still live in communities scattered across northern New Mexico and northeastern Arizona, including many famed pueblos in New Mexico's Rio Grande Valley.

CARLSBAD CAVERNS NATIONAL PARK

DESIGNATED A NATIONAL PARK IN 1930 and a World Heritage Site in 1995, Carlsbad Caverns ranks among the best-known and most popular caves on Earth. Yet even its considerable fame cannot prepare a first-time visitor for the extraordinary array of beautiful and diverse formations that await along its miles of underground passageways. From massive columns that dwarf people standing nearby to delicate, tenuous "soda straws" more slender than a child's finger, Carlsbad's rooms and corridors offer an endless succession of delights.

Understanding the creation of all this subterranean beauty requires a trip back in time more than 240 million years, when what is now southeastern New Mexico was covered by a shallow subtropical sea. A huge horseshoe-shaped reef formed in the warm water, eventually transforming into limestone. Buried by later sediments, this ancient fossil reef was then uplifted by tectonic forces; large subsurface chambers were dissolved by water made acidic by petroleum deposits.

In the past few million years, water dripping into the cave through cracks in its limestone "roof" deposited calcite (crystalized calcium carbonate) as the awe-inspiring variety of cave formations present today. The terrain above the cave is now part of the Chihuahuan Desert, receiving about 14 inches of precipitation a year—a very different climate than that prevailing here during periods such as the most recent ice age, when higher rainfall supported pine forests over the cave. As a result, little water seeps into the cave now, and the rate of creation of new formations has slowed to a standstill.

There are two ways to enter Carlsbad Caverns. Visitors with the physical ability and time should walk through the huge rock arch called the Natural Entrance. The route taken by the earliest explorers in the late 19th century, the path has been paved but still descends 750 feet in 1.25 miles to reach the Big Room. Along the way, walkers pass sights such as the Devil's Spring, where a multi-layered column rises from a placid pool of water, and the Witch's Finger, a slender stalagmite that gives the impression of having twisted as it formed. The path passes by Iceberg Rock, a 200,000-ton boulder that fell from the cave ceiling thousands of years ago.

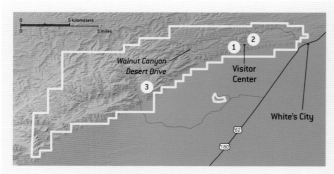

CARLSBAD CAVERNS NEW MEXICO

AREA
46,766 acres (189 sq km)

ESTABLISHED
May 1930

VISITOR INFORMATION
(575) 785 2232;
www.nps.gov/cave

KEY ATTRACTIONS ① Carlsbad Caverns ② Natural Entrance ③ Slaughter Cave

NOTABLE WILDLIFE Mule deer, pronghorn, collared peccary, coyote, Brazilian free-tailed bat, cave swallow

Giant Dome (center) and Twin Domes (right) are features on the Big Room route, a 1-mile, self-guided walk around the perimeter of the largest room (8.2 acres) in Carlsbad Caverns. The most popular tour in the cave, the path passes famed locations such as Bottomless Pit, Rock of Ages, and Painted Grotto.

In addition to its underground wonders, the national park protects a significant expanse of the northern Chihuahuan Desert, the wettest and most biologically diverse desert in the western hemisphere. Among the Chihuahuan Desert's varied flora are more species of cactus than are found in any of the world's other deserts.

From spring through fall, visitors gather at the Natural Entrance at dusk to watch the exit flight of hundreds of thousands of Brazilian free-tailed bats, which leave the cave to feed on nocturnal insects. The bats migrate to their wintering grounds in Mexico by late October and return in March and April.

An alternative entry descends to the Big Room via elevator, making it accessible for visitors with physical limitations. Once here (by elevator or the Natural Entrance route), visitors can take a self-guided 1-mile walk around this massive chamber, covering an estimated 8.2 acres and home to some of the cave's most famous formations. Among them are the Hall of the Giants, with huge stalagmites looming above the path; the Chinese Theater, with a vaguely pagoda-shaped formation; the imposing, multi-tiered Rock of Ages; the Doll's Theater, where thin stalagmites, stalactites, and columns crowd together in an intricate display; and the gorgeous Painted Grotto.

Park rangers offer a selection of guided tours to areas of Carlsbad Caverns away from the popular Big Room. One of the best winds through the Lower Cave, past such formations as the Texas Toothpick, a slender, pointed stalactite more than 10 feet long, and the Rookery, with beautiful clusters of the shiny round calcite objects called cave pearls. The Left Hand Tunnel guided tour proceeds by lantern light, with rangers discussing the cave's history and the fossils of some of the millions of sea creatures found within the limestone that surrounds Carlsbad Caverns.

More than 110 caves have been discovered within the area encompassed by Carlsbad Caverns National Park, although only a few are accessible to the public. In summer, rangers lead tours of Slaughter Canyon Cave, located 23 miles from the park visitor center. Using flashlights, participants walk an unpaved 1.25-mile route past formations such as the Christmas Tree, which resembles a tree partly covered in sparkling snow, and the Monarch, at 89 feet high one of the tallest known cave columns. Even wilder is the Spider Cave tour (Sundays only), which requires crawling and climbing while wearing hard hats, headlamps, kneepads, and gloves.

Between late May and mid-October, around 400,000 Brazilian free-tailed bats roost and raise their young in a side passage of Carlsbad Caverns, leaving at sunset to feed on insects. One of the highlights of a visit to the national park is the daily ranger-led Bat Flight Program, taking place shortly before dusk at the cave's Natural Entrance. After a ranger gives a presentation on the bats' natural history, visitors watch the spectacle of seemingly endless streams of these flying mammals zooming out of the cave, swirling overhead like a dark river in the sky.

A caver makes his way through Lechuguilla Cave, a part of Carlsbad Caverns National Park now known to be the fifth-longest cave in the world and the deepest limestone cave in the United States. Unexplored until the 1980s and in pristine condition, Lechuguilla is open only to scientists and survey teams.

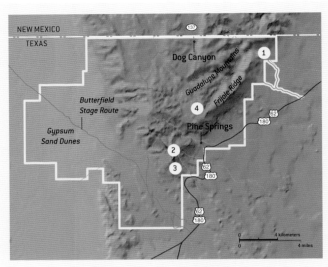

GUADALUPE MOUNTAINS TEXAS

AREA
86,189 acres (349 sq km)

ESTABLISHED
September 1972

VISITOR INFORMATION
(915) 828 3251;
www.nps.gov/gumo

KEY ATTRACTIONS ① McKittrick
Canyon ② Guadalupe Peak
③ El Capitan ④ The Bowl

NOTABLE WILDLIFE Elk, mountain
lion, black bear, collared peccary,
kit fox, badger, peregrine falcon,
mountain chickadee, spotted owl

*An oasis in the desert, McKittrick Canyon is home to riparian woodland of oaks,
hickories, and—most notably—bigtooth maples, which display fall foliage of brilliant
colors. A trail ascends beside McKittrick Creek to reach splendid panoramas of the
Guadalupe Mountains and surrounding desert.*

The imposing profile of El Capitan has long been a landmark for travelers crossing the Chihuahuan Desert. Guadalupe Peak, just to the north, is the highest point in Texas at 8,749 feet. These and all the rest of the limestone Guadalupe Mountains were formed as a gigantic reef in an ancient sea.

GUADALUPE MOUNTAINS NATIONAL PARK

O FTEN OVERSHADOWED BY ITS NEIGHBOR Carlsbad Caverns, less than an hour by highway to the northeast, Guadalupe Mountains National Park richly rewards those who explore its unique blend of desert and mountain habitats. Geologists know the park as the world's best example of a fossilized reef; biologists recognize it as a home for plants and animals rare or unknown elsewhere in Texas; while the casual traveler marvels at a landscape of striking beauty, with imposing peaks, wooded canyons, and lush, spring-fed oases.

The park's most immediately impressive feature is the mountain summit called El Capitan, with sheer cliffs rising abruptly from the Chihuahuan Desert lowland. Once used as a landmark by Native Americans, westbound pioneers, and drivers of the Butterfield Overland Mail stagecoach line, El Capitan dominates views from many directions—although it is not the highest peak in the park. That honor goes to 8,749-foot Guadalupe Peak, the highest point in Texas, which rises just to the north.

Improbable as it seems, these and the rest of the massive Guadalupe Mountains were originally formed more than 200 million years ago as a reef in a shallow sea, built of the remains of countless life forms such as sponges, bryozoans (tiny colonial animals that build stony skeletons of calcium carbonate), and algae. Fossil marine creatures can still be seen within the Guadalupes, which are raised high now as the result of tectonic movements and ancient episodes of mountain uplift.

The most popular, and arguably the most beautiful, site within the national park is McKittrick Canyon, located in the northeastern corner. Following spring-fed McKittrick Creek upstream, a trail climbs from the desert vegetation of cactus, agave, and mesquite into woodland of pine, juniper, and oak, with rock walls towering hundreds of feet overhead. The canyon is especially known for Texas madrone, with peeling reddish bark, and bigtooth maple, which attracts crowds of visitors in fall with its brilliant foliage, ranging from yellow to red and orange. Hikers who continue high enough will come upon spectacular ridgetop vistas across the rugged, rocky Guadalupes and on over the surrounding desert.

Many visitors eagerly undertake the strenuous 4.2-mile (one way) hike to "the top of Texas": the summit of Guadalupe Peak. The panorama here seems to go on forever, including the blindingly white expanse of gypsum sand dunes to the west. Another challenging hike leads to the Bowl, a high-elevation area of ridges and canyons where ponderosa pine and Douglas-fir grow, creating an environment more like the Rocky Mountains than the western Texas desert country.

A much easier hike, the Devil's Hall Trail leads up Pine Spring Canyon under tall cliffs rising steeply on both sides. The most notable feature of the route is the Hiker's Staircase, a natural rock staircase on the way to the narrow gorge called Devil's Hall.

The Rio Grande forms the southern boundary of Big Bend National Park, named for the curving course of this section of the river. Riparian areas along the Rio Grande comprise one of the three major park ecosystems; the others are the highlands of the Chisos Mountains and the expanse of the Chihuahuan Desert.

BIG BEND NATIONAL PARK

THE SCENERY OF BIG BEND NATIONAL PARK is so spectacular, and spread over such a vast area, that a first-time visitor could spend days simply trying to take it all in. Yet the visual appeal of the rugged landscape is only one reason why this park ranks as a favorite among those who make the long drive across the western Texas desert to see it.

Rangers like to say that Big Bend is three parks in one, based on its three major ecosystems: an expansive area of Chihuahuan Desert, a narrow band of riparian vegetation along the Rio Grande, and the forested highlands of the Chisos Mountains at the heart of the park. The juxtaposition of these very different habitats creates a diversity of plants and animals unparalleled among America's national parks. In addition, Big Bend boasts a complex and fascinating geological history, a story plainly displayed in its multifaceted rock formations for those who take time to appreciate it.

The park takes its name from the "big bend" that the Rio Grande makes in western Texas as it flows from New Mexico toward the Gulf of Mexico, looping south and then back north. The park's southern border coincides with 118 miles of the river, which also forms the border between the United States and Mexico. This is demanding country, with little rainfall and a terrain that made travel difficult in the days before highways. Apart from scattered ranches and a few mines, it has seen little human presence over the years.

No matter which of the two entrances to the park a traveler uses, getting to any of the developed areas requires a long drive across the Chihuahuan Desert, the habitat that makes up 98 percent of Big Bend. For much of the year it is a place of sparse plant growth and low hills studded with countless boulders and rock outcrops. Yet in spring, after sufficient precipitation, this desert landscape bursts into color as

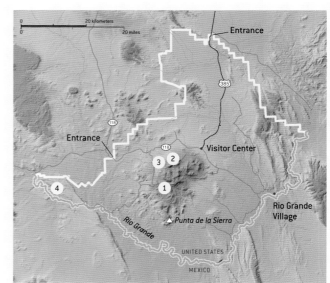

BIG BEND TEXAS

AREA
801,163 acres (3,242 sq km)
ESTABLISHED
June 1944
VISITOR INFORMATION
(432) 477 2251;
www.nps.gov/bibe

KEY ATTRACTIONS ① Chisos Mountains ② The Basin ③ The Window ④ Santa Elena Canyon
NOTABLE WILDLIFE Mountain lion, black bear, mule deer, white-tailed deer, collared peccary, Colima warbler, zone-tailed hawk

wildflowers and shrubs bloom in profusion. Among the blossoms are those of dozens of species of cacti, which Big Bend has in greater variety than any other national park.

Looming in the distance are the imposing peaks of the Chisos Mountains, formed from volcanic eruptions and magma flows more than 40 million years ago and eroded into steep bluffs, deep canyons, and a superb collection of oddly shaped rock formations. At the mountains' northern edge is the park's main visitor center at Panther Junction, with a nearby short nature trail identifying common desert plants.

There is only one road into the Chisos, a route up Green Gulch that twists and turns to reach the rim of the Basin, the great bowl-shaped area in the center of the mountains. The skyline here is dominated by the magnificent sheer-sided summit called Casa Grande. Rising even higher is 7,825-foot Emory Peak, the park's highest point.

Renowned for their biological diversity and for the contrast they offer to the surrounding desert, the Chisos Mountains are home to black bears and mountain lions, which roam through woodland of oaks, Douglas-fir, quaking aspen, bigtooth maple, and ponderosa pine. The most sought-after animal in the mountains is a small gray-and-yellow bird called the Colima warbler, which nests here and nowhere else in the United States.

Many popular trails begin in the Basin, including hikes to Boot Canyon, where erosion has created a tall rock formation looking exactly like an upside-down boot, and to the Window, a narrow slot in the Basin wall. More adventurous hikers can head farther afield to areas such as the South Rim. Here at the southern edge of the High Chisos, the trail runs along an escarpment 2,500 feet above the desert below, and fabulous panoramic views extend beyond the Rio Grande into Mexico.

No visitor can fail to notice the amazing blooms of the Havard agave, also known as the century plant, which grows commonly on Chisos Mountain slopes. The flower stalk rises as high as 15 feet, holding candelabra-like clusters of bright yellow flowers attractive to hummingbirds. This showy display happens only once, when the plant is 20 to 40 years old, after

A charismatic bird of arid regions, the greater roadrunner rarely flies, instead running swiftly with long, strong legs in pursuit of lizards, small snakes, large insects, and other prey. Roadrunners, members of the cuckoo family, are seen frequently around campgrounds in Big Bend National Park.

which the agave dies. A related species, lechuguilla, is an indicator plant of the Chihuahuan Desert—that is, one that grows only in that ecoregion.

On the southern border of the park, the Rio Grande flows placidly beside low banks in places, while in other areas it has carved canyons of awesome depth. Santa Elena Canyon, in the southwestern part of the park, can be reached via the Ross Maxwell Scenic Drive. Meandering through the desert west of the Chisos Mountains, this route passes dikes of volcanic magma intrusions and the picturesque landmark called Mule Ears Peaks before reaching the river near the Castolon Visitor Center. Farther west, a short trail allows hikers to enter breathtaking Santa Elena Canyon, where the Rio Grande flows under cliffs up to 1,500 feet high. Rafters, kayakers, and canoeists are seen often here, having completed a trip through the canyon, which at times features rapids up to Class IV.

Boquillas Canyon, in the southeastern part of Big Bend, offers further boating opportunities, with rapids only to Class II. Here, as at Santa Elena, a short trail allows hikers to get a glimpse of the canyon. Boaters who enter Boquillas will find no takeout sites for the next 33 miles. The trail is located just east of Rio Grande Village, a popular campground and a favorite destination for birdwatchers. The park's third canyon, Mariscal, in the far southern portion of the park, is more difficult to access, reached only by a long, rough, unpaved road. Experienced hikers and boaters maintain that the canyon's beauty and grandeur make the trip well worth the effort.

River, desert, and mountain, Big Bend's "three parks" provide endless opportunities for travelers, from scenic drives to strenuous long-distance hiking trips across rugged terrain. For naturalists and adventurers, no national park offers more.

This claret cup cactus is one of dozens of species of wildflowers that can turn the Chihuahuan Desert into a wonderland of color after winters and early springs with adequate precipitation, and again in late summer after the annual "monsoon" rainy season. Most cacti bloom in mid- to late spring.

ARCHES
NATIONAL PARK

ARCHES NATIONAL PARK EXEMPLIFIES much of the iconic landscape associated with the American Southwest: expansive areas of rugged, rocky terrain, studded with picturesque buttes, pinnacles, and canyons composed of the colorful sandstone that makes up much of the "red-rock country" of the Colorado Plateau region.

Yet it is an additional feature of the terrain that led to the creation of a national park here, and gave the park its name: more than 2,000 natural rock arches, the greatest collection of these graceful geological features on Earth. Some soaring high in elongated, tenuous shapes, others squat and low to the ground, they range from 3 feet wide or tall (the smallest size considered a true arch) to Landscape Arch, which spans 306 feet from foot to foot. The beautiful Delicate Arch possesses such a distinctive form that it has been featured on vehicle license plates as a symbol of the State of Utah. (The park calls Delicate Arch "the best-known arch in the world.")

An 18-mile scenic drive winds through the heart of Arches National Park, providing access to side roads, lookout points, and trailheads leading to much of the best park scenery. Although it might seem possible to quickly traverse such a short road, in fact a traveler would need days to thoroughly explore all its features.

Opportunities to enjoy the park's highlights come soon after heading north from the visitor center, with the trailhead for the magnificent canyon known as Park Avenue. Along one side stand tall cliffs topped with "fins" that rise like elaborate ornamentation, while the imposing formation called Courthouse Towers, with a near architectural structure, stands

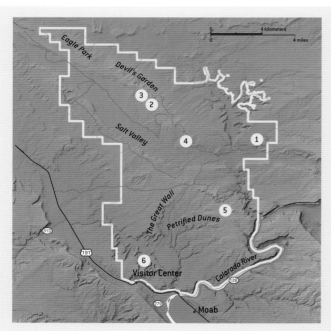

ARCHES UTAH

AREA
76,519 acres (309 sq km)

ESTABLISHED
November 1971

VISITOR INFORMATION
(435) 719 2299;
www.nps.gov/arch

KEY ATTRACTIONS ① Delicate Arch ② Landscape Arch ③ Double Arch ④ Fiery Furnace ⑤ The Windows ⑥ Park Avenue

NOTABLE WILDLIFE Desert bighorn sheep, mule deer, mountain lion, black-tailed jackrabbit, ringtail cat

Delicate Arch is the most famous of the more than 2,000 examples of this geological feature in Arches National Park. Photographing Delicate Arch's beautiful form at sunrise or sunset has long been among the park's most popular off-road activities. The snow-capped La Sal Mountains provide a contrasting background to the scene.

nearby. A short distance down the road is a viewpoint looking toward the La Sal Mountains to the southeast. Their summits, snow-capped for much of the year, provide a vivid contrast to the stark surrounding landscape.

Farther along the road stand more of the park's famous sights, including the Organ, which resembles a pipe organ; Sheep Rock, which has a top outline that does indeed resemble that animal; and the Three Gossips, which give the impression of a trio of figures standing together to exchange news. Passing the aptly named Great Wall, the road arrives at the amazing Balanced Rock, where a huge boulder seems precariously perched on a leaning column.

The shapes and sizes of the park's pinnacles, hoodoos, and other formations appear infinite in variety, their appearance often enhanced by layers and striations. Almost all the park's major geological features are composed of Entrada Sandstone, a rock widespread in the West that was deposited as sedimentary material more than 140 million years ago, and even older Navajo Sandstone.

Just beyond Balanced Rock is the side road to the park's Windows Section, a wonderland of arches and other scenic highlights. Among these are Double Arch, two large arches joined at one end, and the Windows, where a 1-mile trail leads to three even larger arches: North Window, South Window, and Turret. One group of humpbacked formations in the Windows area has been given an especially evocative name: Parade of Elephants.

Four miles up the main park road from the Windows turnoff is the road offering access to Delicate Arch. There are two ways to see this beautiful formation, which stands on a slope amid pyramidal rock stacks and mini-mesas. A short trail at the end of the side road leads to a viewpoint of Delicate Arch 1 mile distant. To see the arch up close requires hiking a 3-mile round trip from the Wolfe Ranch trailhead. Lacking any shade, this popular route should be avoided on hot days except early in the morning or late in the afternoon. Along the way, the route passes over an extensive area of the nearly featureless terrain called slickrock, where hikers must watch for rock cairns to stay on the path.

Ahead on the main road is the spectacular area called Fiery Furnace, a maze of tall, red sandstone pinnacles and fins. Best visited on a ranger-led hike—some park visitors have got lost inside this fantastic geological jumble—this site features narrow passageways, dead-end canyons, and moderately strenuous rock-scrambling through an area that seems a showcase for the power of erosion on rock.

The paved road ends at the Devil's Garden area, gateway to some of the park's most popular formations. Among them are two arches that have, in relatively recent times, demonstrated the continually evolving nature of the park landscape. Skyline

The best way to explore the park's Fiery Furnace area is on a ranger-led tour. This maze of fins, spires, and narrow passageways can quickly lead to disorientation for hikers. Those who want to enter Fiery Furnace on their own must first watch a video on safety and resource protection.

A sunflower called rough mules-ears blooms in the Courthouse Towers area, which includes some of the most striking rock formations in the park. Even in this desert terrain, plants from tiny mosses to pinyon pines and junipers find ways to survive.

Seeming to defy the forces of gravity and erosion, Balanced Rock endures as one of the most striking geological formations in Arches National Park. Differing resistance to weathering by rock strata creates an endless variety of shapes, from spires to arches.

The imposing formations of Park Avenue demonstrate the fantastic array of shapes that erosion has sculpted in Arches National Park. Narrow fins often erode into solitary pinnacles or weaken to the point of collapse, but under the right conditions an opening may form that eventually widens into an arch.

Two formidable arches share a common base at famed Double Arch, reached via an easy quarter-mile trail.

Arch, visible from the road and reached by an easy, short trail, had its opening double in size in 1940 when a large section of rock fell. Landscape Arch also changed shape when a huge slab of rock fell in 1991, making this fragile-looking arch seem even more delicate.

Over time, all the arches present today in Arches National Park will cease to exist, as water, ice, and wind-blown grit continue their work. In 2008, Wall Arch, then the 12th-largest arch in the park, collapsed almost completely. Its remains can be seen along the Devil's Garden trail beyond Landscape Arch. Farther along the trail, which becomes increasingly difficult, are several other formations, including Double O Arch, where a small arch nestles beneath a far larger opening in a rock wall.

Another draw of the park are the desert bighorn sheep that can sometimes be spotted near the visitor center. Once approaching extinction because of disease and overhunting, these mammals, with the males' massive curving horns, have made a slow comeback thanks to reintroduction efforts. Bighorn now number several dozen in the park.

CANYONLANDS NATIONAL PARK

SPLENDID AND VARIED EXAMPLES OF America's emblematic southwestern landscape are protected within Canyonlands National Park, a place especially appealing to travelers with a spirit of adventure. From overlooks here, panoramas take in vast areas of flat-topped buttes, tall rock spires, bizarrely eroded hoodoos, graceful arches, and deeply incised canyons, in hues from brown to yellow to deep red. The Colorado and Green Rivers meet in the center of the park, with steep-sided gorges marking their courses both above and below their confluence.

Relatively few paved roads lead into the heart of the 527-square-mile park, which means that much of its spectacular terrain is in essence reserved for hikers, mountain-bikers, boaters, and drivers with high-clearance vehicles. Travel here can be demanding: less than 10 inches of rain falls annually, summers are very hot, winters are cold, and the temperature can vary nearly 50°F (30°C) in a single day. Yet for those who relish solitude, who prepare well, and who appreciate the stark magnificence of the Colorado Plateau, Canyonlands offers limitless possibilities for exploration.

The canyons of the Green and Colorado Rivers, which meet in a Y shape, divide the park into four sections: Island in the Sky, a high-altitude mesa between the forks of the Y; the Needles, to the east; the Maze, to the west; and the rivers themselves,

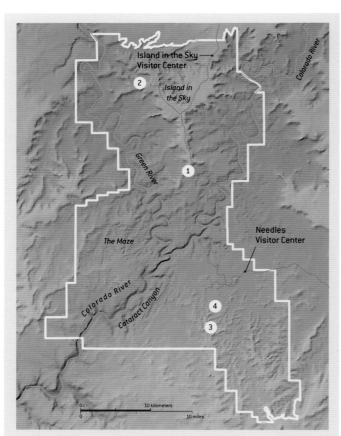

CANYONLANDS UTAH

AREA
337,598 acres (1,365 sq km)
ESTABLISHED
September 1964
VISITOR INFORMATION
(435) 719 2313;
www.nps.gov/cany

KEY ATTRACTIONS ① Grand View Point ② Upheaval Dome ③ The Needles ④ Elephant Hill
NOTABLE WILDLIFE Desert bighorn sheep, mule deer, mountain lion, black bear, beaver, spotted owl, pinyon jay

Colorful and weirdly shaped rock formations highlight the Needles section of Canyonlands National Park, shaped by erosion of red and white sandstone. Shallow eroded basins known as ephemeral pools are home to ecosystems in miniature, where plants and animals have adapted to a harsh environment.

Desert bighorn sheep from Canyonlands have been used for reintroduction programs elsewhere in the American Southwest. Once on the path to extinction these mammals have made a comeback and, while not nearly as common as they once were, now number an estimated 3,000 in Utah.

including the Colorado's Cataract Canyon, long a favorite whitewater trip for rafters. Most park development is located in the Island in the Sky district, where stunning views of geological features can be enjoyed from roadside sites or along relatively easy trails. The Needles is reached by a paved road, but hiking or backcountry driving is required to see the best of its attractions. The Maze is very remote, with few developed areas, and requires several days and careful preparation for a rewarding visit. No roads directly connect the park's three land districts.

Entering the Island in the Sky district from the north, travelers soon reach the main visitor center and the overlook into Shafer Canyon, a valley bordered by high cliffs of reddish sandstone. Farther south, a short trail leads to Mesa Arch, set on a cliff edge and with fabulous views through its rock "window." A turn to the northwest here leads to some of the park's most famous sites, such as the Green River Overlook, a vista of near endless canyons and mesas, and Upheaval Dome, a circular geological feature of still debated origin. The road south ends at Grand View Point Overlook, where an easy 1-mile trail leads to the very edge of the Island in the Sky mesa and a vista ranking among the park's best.

The scenic highlight of the Needles district is the Needles themselves, a crowded formation of tall spires with odd bulging shapes in shades of red and tan. Legendary Elephant Hill is a challenging climb for four-wheel-drive vehicles and mountain bikes, with tight turns and extremely steep sections of slickrock.

West of the main park, the Horseshoe Canyon Unit is best known for the Great Gallery, where Native Americans painted large figures in intricate designs. Reaching the pictograph site requires a 3.2-mile (one way) hike through a scenic canyon with high vertical sandstone walls.

CAPITOL REEF
NATIONAL PARK

STRETCHING FOR 100 MILES ACROSS THE desert of south-central Utah is a massive warp in the Earth's crust, a fold in the underlying rocks that geologists call a monocline. Created more than 50 million years ago, the fold was uplifted and exposed by later erosion, resulting in a spectacular north–south line of colorful cliffs, canyons, and rock formations, a terrain where each turn along a trail brings new and varied geological wonders. This dramatic feature is named Waterpocket Fold, for the "pockets" of water that collect in naturally eroded pits or basins in the sandstone rock predominant in the area.

Ancestral Puebloan people of the Fremont culture lived here, and left petroglyphs recording their lives. European-American explorers found the long line of cliffs and called one section Capitol Reef, for the white sandstone domes resembling the U.S. Capitol building, and for the way the cliffs impeded travel like a reef in the ocean.

Travelers today encounter Capitol Reef National Park at the historic townsite of Fruita, along the Fremont River, where early settlers created a community of orchards and gardens amid the surrounding desert. Visitors can see a farmstead, schoolhouse, blacksmith shop, and 2,700 fruit and nut trees remaining from the pioneer era.

Several park attractions are found near Fruita and along Utah Highway 24, including Goosenecks Overlook, a vista of dramatically deep and convoluted canyons cut into the red rock by Sulphur Creek, and Hickman Bridge, a huge natural rock arch. Among the evocative rock formations near Fruita are Capitol Dome, a rounded hill of light-buff sandstone; the Castle, an imposing crenellated peak; and Chimney Rock, a beautifully fluted red-rock wall.

A 10-mile scenic drive leads south from the park Visitor Center along the west face of Capitol Reef, bringing close looks at multicolored cliffs of sandstone, shale, and volcanic ash. Side roads lead into Grand Wash and Capitol Gorge, steep-sided ravines with awe-inspiring scenery within their narrow, twisting courses. An available road guide provides an instructive lesson in the geological processes that created this terrain.

A longer, less-developed road leads into Cathedral Valley, in the northern part of the park, home to some of the finest panoramas in the region. Banded cliffs border flat valleys studded with spires and monoliths with names such as Jailhouse Rock, the Temple of the Sun, and Wall of Jericho. "Cathedral" is an apt name for this district, where many of the soaring formations do indeed resemble Gothic church architecture.

The remote southern section of the park is reached by the Notom-Bullfrog Road, running parallel to the east side of Waterpocket Fold. The unpaved Burr Trail Road climbs and crosses the fold via a dramatic series of tight switchbacks, offering fine views of the surrounding landscape.

The dramatic and colorful sandstone walls of Capitol Gorge rank with the most beautiful scenes in Capitol Reef National Park. Pioneer settlers built a road through the gorge in 1884, and the route remained in use until 1962. Modern travelers should avoid entering the narrow canyon if flash flooding is possible.

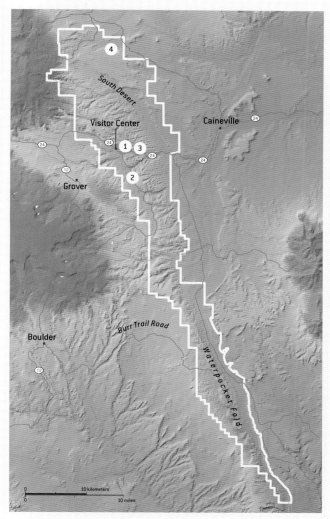

CAPITOL REEF UTAH

AREA
241,234 acres (976 sq km)

ESTABLISHED
December 1971

VISITOR INFORMATION
(435) 425 3791;
www.nps.gov/care

KEY ATTRACTIONS ① Historic Fruita ② Scenic Drive ③ Hickman Bridge ④ Cathedral Valley

NOTABLE WILDLIFE Mule deer, mountain lion, porcupine, gray fox, ringtail cat, badger

The fruit of the prickly pear cactus was widely used for food by Native Americans, as were the pads (after spines were picked or burned off). With an average of around 7 inches of precipitation (both rain and snow) a year, Capitol Reef lies on the edge of the Great Basin Desert ecoregion.

Two species of yuccas (in the agave family) are found in Capitol Reef National Park. Their waxy whitish flowers are pollinated only by small moths, which lay their eggs in the blooms. The moth larvae feed on yucca seeds. The sharp-pointed leaves of one species of yucca led to the common name Spanish bayonet.

The Gilford Barn is part of the community of Fruita, a Mormon settlement that began around 1880 and never comprised more than ten families. Fruita was known for its orchards of cherry, apricot, peach, pear, apple, and other trees, which still exist and bear fruit, available for harvest by park visitors for a small fee.

BRYCE CANYON NATIONAL PARK

EVEN IN THE CONTEXT OF AMERICA'S endlessly varied and spectacular national parks, Bryce Canyon is renowned for its beauty. Here on the eastern edge of the Paunsaugunt Plateau, erosion has created a wonderland of rock formations arrayed across natural amphitheaters in limestone cliff faces. Pinnacles, fins, spires, arches, windows, walls, mesas, buttes—the names are endless, and so are the multitudinous shapes and colors of these formations, crowded together to form mazes that both invite and resist exploration. Ebenezer Bryce, the 19th-century pioneer whose name became associated with this area, is said to have described the terrain as "a hell of a place to lose a cow."

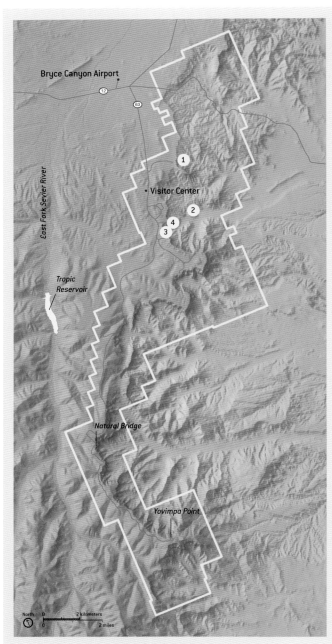

BRYCE CANYON UTAH

AREA
35,835 acres (145 sq km)
ESTABLISHED
February 1928
VISITOR INFORMATION
(435) 834 5322;
www.nps.gov/brca

KEY ATTRACTIONS ① Fairyland Canyon ② Bryce Canyon ③ Wall Street ④ Thor's Hammer
NOTABLE WILDLIFE Mule deer, Utah prairie dog, gray fox, pronghorn, elk, wild turkey, peregrine falcon, California condor

The famed hoodoos of Bryce Canyon National Park form as a plateau erodes into a narrow fin, which further weathers into a series of adjoining columns. Eventually windows form between columns, which are later left isolated as free-standing spires. Differing resistance of rock layers contributes to a hoodoo's varying diameter.

From one of the park's popular lookouts such as Fairyland Point or Bryce Point, the jumble of spires below creates a dizzying scene. Bryce Canyon is known for the bizarrely shaped formations called hoodoos: slender vertical rock columns whose thickness varies along their height, giving them silhouettes that can bring to mind humans, animals, mythological creatures, architectural forms, and other images limited only by the observer's resourceful mind. The Paiute Native Americans who once lived in this region saw hoodoos as ancient people who had been transformed into rock.

Nearly all this fantastic terrain was created by the weathering action of water freezing and thawing. Precipitation collects within cracks, and as it freezes into ice it expands, exerting tremendous force to split rocks repeatedly into smaller and smaller sections. (Bryce Canyon National Park experiences more than 200 days a year when the temperature rises above and drops below freezing.) Rain—though scant in this high desert country—also plays a part in erosion. The minute amount of acid in rainfall slowly dissolves limestone, smoothing the edges of rock formations and making them rounder and less jagged.

An 18-mile scenic road leads along the top of the Paunsaugunt Plateau, entering the park in the north and ending at Rainbow Point in the south. The drive features 13 viewpoints overlooking various locations along the cliff edge. The park encompasses an elevation difference of more than 2,000 feet, which contributes not only to its geological splendor but to the diversity of its flora and fauna. Fir, spruce, and aspen grow in high elevations, with ponderosa pine and manzanita in middle levels and dry juniper-pinyon pine forest at low elevations.

Shortly after the main drive enters the park, a 1-mile side road leads to Fairyland Point and the vista into Fairyland Canyon, where hoodoos are almost at eye level. Geologically younger than the formations to the south, these hoodoos seem bulkier and less sculpted than those in other sections. Beyond the park visitor center is a loop road to famed Sunrise Point, where countless pink-and-buff hoodoos create one of Bryce Canyon's most iconic panoramas. In the distance is Boat Mesa and the huge tilted rock slab called Sinking Ship. Sunrise Point and Bryce Point, to the south, are favorite sites to watch dawn's

Prairie dogs are rodents related to squirrels that live in large colonies called towns. Once abundant throughout the West, they have declined in the face of massive extermination campaigns by ranchers. The Utah prairie dog, found in Bryce Canyon, is a federally designated threatened species.

light, while rangers recommend Inspiration Point and Paria View (even more than Sunset Point) for enjoying sunsets.

Sunrise, Sunset, Inspiration, and Bryce Points all overlook Bryce Canyon, not truly a canyon but one of more than a dozen semicircular amphitheaters eroded into the Paunsaugunt Plateau. The view from Sunset is dominated by the tall hoodoo named Thor's Hammer, while the collection of hoodoos called Silent City is visible from many locations along the rim.

Although vistas from the plateau rim are spectacular, seeing the true glory of Bryce Canyon requires hiking down among the hoodoos on some of the park's trails. Doing so allows close looks at areas such as Wall Street (a narrow slot canyon), Queen's Garden, and Hat Shop (with many balanced-rock formations). Exploring areas below the rim also permits hikers to reach hoodoos with such evocative names as Tower Bridge (an exquisitely turreted natural window in a rock wall), Indian Princess, and Queen Victoria.

To the south of Bryce Point, Paria View is known as a good wildlife-viewing location. Mule deer, elk, pronghorn, and peregrine falcons may be seen from here at times. Birdwatching is also good at the next viewpoint south, Swamp Canyon. A trail here leads into an area much wetter than the rest of the park, with creeks and a spring supporting diverse vegetation.

The aptly named Farview overlook offers vistas stretching well over 100 miles, taking in the Kaiparowits Plateau and the conical hill called Molly's Nipple. Bryce Canyon National Park is famed for its lack of air pollution and excellent long-distance views. High air quality and clear skies make it a favorite destination for astronomy buffs. Farview is in the transition zone between ponderosa pine forests to the north and blue spruce and Douglas-fir woodlands on higher ground to the south.

The scenic road then passes the viewpoint for Natural Bridge, an impressive window in a rock wall tinted red by iron oxide. Technically speaking, this "bridge" is really an arch, because it was created by weathering and not by a stream flowing through it.

At Yovimpa Point, the park's southernmost overlook, visitors can observe the many rock strata that make up the Grand Staircase, the geological sequence of sedimentary layers stretching south to the Grand Canyon. One layer, the Pink Cliffs, provides the material for Bryce Canyon's hoodoos. Below are arrayed the Gray, White, Vermilion, and Chocolate Cliffs. Yovimpa Point is one of the very few places where multiple layers of the Grand Staircase can be seen. The view provides a graphic lesson in the geology of the Colorado Plateau, dating back in time more than 600 million years.

ZION NATIONAL PARK

THERE ARE THOSE WHO BELIEVE THAT Zion is the most beautiful of America's national parks, and though debate on the issue can never be resolved, Zion's advocates have plenty of evidence to back up their case. The work of erosion and weathering on the sedimentary rock of the Colorado Plateau has created a place where multicolored peaks and cliffs rise high above narrow canyons; a dramatic landscape whose visual aspect changes with the slant of sunlight throughout the day. The names of park features themselves give an idea of the awe-inspiring nature of the terrain: Court of the Patriarchs, the Great White Throne, the Sentinel, Mountain of Mystery.

Zion National Park lies in the middle of the Grand Staircase, a series of rock layers that form figurative "steps" between the Grand Canyon in Arizona and Bryce Canyon in Utah. Much of the rock in Zion is sandstone, originally dunes of an ancient desert, formed into rock and tinted shades of red by iron oxide.

When the Colorado Plateau was uplifted over millions of years, the Virgin River and its tributaries cut deeply into the Earth, forming both wide valleys and extremely narrow gorges called slot canyons. Zion Canyon, the heart of the national park, was formed by the North Fork of the Virgin River, which also cut the upper canyon area called the Narrows, perhaps the most famous slot canyon in the country.

From the south entrance of the park, Zion Canyon Scenic Drive winds 6 miles north, providing access to many of Zion's most

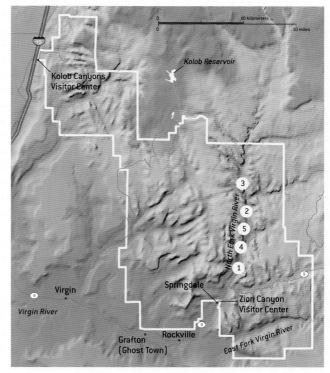

ZION UTAH

AREA
148,199 acres (600 sq km)

ESTABLISHED
November 1919

VISITOR INFORMATION
(435) 772 3256;
www.nps.gov/zion

KEY ATTRACTIONS ① Zion Canyon
② Temple of Sinawava ③ The
Narrows ④ Emerald Pools
⑤ Angels Landing

NOTABLE WILDLIFE Mountain lion,
mule deer, elk, bighorn sheep, wild
turkey, California condor

Their foliage turning yellow in autumn, Fremont cottonwoods cover the valley of the North Fork of the Virgin River in the vicinity of the Zion National Park lodge. Tall, eroded bluffs of reddish sandstone tower over the scene, part of the rock layers that have come to be called the Grand Staircase.

North of the Temple of Sinawava, the North Fork of the Virgin River and other streams have carved narrow gorges in the relatively soft sandstone of Zion National Park. Called slot canyons, these steep-sided chasms offer thrilling hiking, but can turn dangerous quickly when rains bring flash floods.

One of the world's fastest birds, the peregrine falcon declined dramatically in population because of persecution and pesticide use in the mid-20th century, but has made an encouraging comeback in recent decades. The cliffs of Zion National Park create perfect nesting habitat for this powerful raptor

Mountain lions, also known as cougars or pumas, are uncommon in Zion but range throughout the park, preying mainly on mule deer. These big cats are usually shy around humans, but hikers should know what to do in case of an encounter. Rangers ask visitors to report sightings of mountain lions.

popular destinations. To relieve traffic congestion, private vehicles are banned within the canyon from spring through fall, with shuttle buses running every few minutes and stopping at trailheads and other attractions.

Looming high over the entrance to Zion Canyon on the west is the imposing bulk of the Sentinel, a peak of reddish sandstone with lighter banding. Slightly farther north rise the three pointed summits called the Court of the Patriarchs. A short walk here leads to a fine lookout spot for these and other peaks. At least one waterfall, and sometimes more depending on recent rains, can be found along the trails in the Emerald Pools area, a beautiful hike into a side canyon.

While views from the floor of Zion Canyon can be spectacular, the panoramas from high points within the park are even more stunning. One of the most popular hikes in the park is the strenuous 2.4-mile ascent to the viewpoint called Angels Landing. Climbing steeply along the tight switchbacks known as Walter's Wiggles, the trail rises more than 1,400 feet—occasionally along extremely narrow rock ridges—to reward hikers with vast vistas of the Virgin River far below, bordered by the sheer cliffs that it has carved over millennia.

Another well-used trail leads a half-mile to Weeping Rock, where tenuous waterfalls drip into a steep-sided alcove, providing moisture for a hanging garden of vegetation. Also beginning here is a far more adventurous trek, the 4-mile hike to Observation Point, which gains 2,148 feet in elevation and passes through narrow Echo Canyon on its way to a perch at the edge of a tall, sheer cliff face. The fabulous vista down Zion Canyon is considered by many to be the best in the park: long lines of red cliffs towering over the green ribbon of trees lining the Virgin River at their bases.

As rewarding as these and other Zion Canyon hikes are, the highlight for many visitors is the area at the northern end of the scenic drive, beginning with the massive line of red-rock cliffs called the Temple of Sinawava. From this impressive scene, the Riverside Walk follows the Virgin

River upstream for a mile to reach the awesome slot canyon called the Narrows. Here, sensuously curved walls crowd in on both sides and rise high overhead, blocking the sun and giving hikers a sense of isolation from the world outside. Often the only trail is the river itself, requiring wading in the cold water. As is the case in all slot canyons, hikers must be aware of the dangers of flash floods, which can turn tranquil creeks into raging torrents in a matter of minutes, trapping those caught inside.

Though Zion Canyon attracts the great majority of the park's 2.5 million annual visitors, it is not the park's only destination. In the northwestern section of Zion National Park, the Kolob Canyons area includes a 5-mile scenic drive and several excellent trails. The most renowned is the 7-mile hike to magnificent Kolob Arch, following Timber Creek and La Verkin Creek under canyon walls as colorful as any in the park. Kolob Arch, a massive structure of pinkish sandstone spanning more than 300 feet, ranks among the largest natural rock arches in the world. An easier hike is the 2.5-mile trail to beautiful Double Arch Alcove, an amphitheater of red and buff rock with overhanging sides that form an intimate grotto. At the end of the scenic drive, a half-mile trail follows a ridgeline to a summit with splendid views over the canyons and peaks of the entire Kolob Canyons region.

The Zion-Mount Carmel Highway, which leads into the park from the east, is an adventure in itself. The road passes the oddly striated peak called Checkerboard Mesa, which shows crossbedding from 200-million-year-old sand dunes, and then winds down Pine Creek Canyon to reach the trailhead for the Canyon Overlook Trail. This half-mile hike ends at one of the finest views in the national park, a vista that takes in Pine Creek Canyon and lower Zion Canyon, a superb scene of massive rugged cliffs.

The highway then travels 1.1 miles through a tunnel before twisting along a series of switchbacks and turning south through Zion Canyon to the park visitor center. As is true everywhere in the park, traveling this route offers an endless series of some of the Southwest's most breathtaking scenery.

GREAT BASIN NATIONAL PARK

GREAT BASIN NATIONAL PARK IS APTLY named, for it lies in the middle of the Great Basin, a distinctive region of the West out of which no rivers flow. Actually a collection of small basins separated by north–south mountain ranges, the Great Basin is home to streams that either sink into the Earth or drain into lakes from which water evaporates, rather than flows to the sea.

Isolated and receiving relatively few visitors, Great Basin National Park centers on 13,063-foot Wheeler Peak, a strikingly rugged mountain whose craggy features were in part sculpted by glaciers. Its great bulk dominating the landscape for miles around, Wheeler is still home to a single small glacier, one of the southernmost in the United States.

The 12-mile Wheeler Peak Scenic Drive ascends the mountain to end at a campground located on the eastern flank at an elevation of nearly 10,000 feet. At its beginning the road traverses dry habitat of juniper and sagebrush, typical of much of the Great Basin, but as it rises it passes woodland of Engelmann spruce, limber pine, white fir, and Douglas-fir, as if the traveler had suddenly been transported to a region much farther north. The views along the way are magnificent, across Wheeler's stark glacier-shaped slopes and on to the surrounding lowlands.

Great Basin National Park is famed for its groves of bristlecone pines, growing on Wheeler Peak just below the treeline. Often gnarled and twisted by the harsh climatic conditions, these trees can be more than 3,000 years old, and some individuals in the park are probably among the oldest trees on Earth. A fairly strenuous 4.6-mile trail leads through a grove of bristlecone pines and on to a close-up look at the park's lone remaining glacier, set beneath tall, sheer cliffs on the mountain's northeast face. The trailhead can be found on the Wheeler Peak Scenic Drive, not far from the campground.

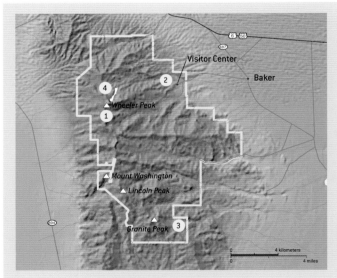

GREAT BASIN NEVADA

AREA
77,180 acres (312 sq km)

ESTABLISHED
October 1986

VISITOR INFORMATION
(775) 234 7331;
www.nps.gov/grba

KEY ATTRACTIONS ① Wheeler Peak ② Lehman Caves ③ Lexington Arch ④ Glacier

NOTABLE WILDLIFE Elk, pronghorn, mountain lion, bighorn sheep, yellow-bellied marmot, greater sage grouse, black rosy-finch

At the opposite extreme from Wheeler Peak's imposing alpine ridges, Great Basin National Park also encompasses more than 40 caves. One, Lehman Caves, can be visited on ranger-led tours, which pass through beautiful marble rooms full of speleothems (cave formations) such as stalagmites, stalactites, flowstones, and hundreds of shield formations, which are common in this cave system and rare elsewhere. Shields—which form at all angles on the ceiling, walls, and floor of the caves—consist of two round or oval parallel plates with a thin crack between them. The shields were formed when water moved through thin fractures in the limestone of the caves, depositing calcite on either side of a narrow water-filled crack.

Much of Great Basin National Park is undeveloped wilderness, offering ample opportunity for hikers to explore the landscape in solitude. In the southern part of the park, a maintained trail leads to Lexington Arch, a 75-foot-high natural arch unusual in that it is made of limestone, not the sandstone of which most Western arches are composed. The road to the Lexington Arch trailhead crosses private property and is primitive and rough: travelers should talk to a park ranger before making the drive. At the end of a 1.7-mile trail, the massive arch looms above Lexington Canyon, its origin still mysterious to geologists.

Lehman Caves, which can be enjoyed on tours led by Great Basin National Park rangers, features a variety of formations from stalagmites and stalactites to shields and draperies. Bodies of sea creatures from an ancient ocean were compressed into limestone, later transformed into the marble that comprises the cave walls.

GRAND CANYON NATIONAL PARK

IN 1869, EXPLORER JOHN WESLEY POWELL LED what is believed to have been the first expedition down the Colorado River through the Grand Canyon. Years later, he wrote that the "glories and the beauties of form, color, and sound unite in the Grand Canyon," and pronounced the landscape he had witnessed to be "the most sublime spectacle in nature."

The glories that thrilled Powell have since been enjoyed by tens of millions of visitors to Grand Canyon National Park, one of the Earth's legendary natural areas. Views from the canyon rim stretch for miles across multicolored cliffs and buttes in an infinitude of shapes. The "sublime spectacle" is the result of 6 million years of erosion on rock that dates back 1.7 billion years. While many travelers simply stand in awe of the beauty before them, geologists have been coming to the Grand Canyon since 1858 to study one of the most complete and important records of the planet's history, written in layers of rock.

Most visitors arrive at the park on the South Rim of the canyon in the vicinity of Grand Canyon Village, where many of the most famous viewpoints are located, including Yavapai Point, Mather Point, and Yaki Point. Among the formations prominent from this area are Zoroaster Temple, Wotan's Throne, and the iconic pointed shape of Isis Temple. The pyramidal shape of the Grand Canyon's "temples" comes from the differing erosion resistance demonstrated by varying types of rock strata.

An important first stop should be the Yavapai Observation Station, which presents easy-to-understand exhibits on the Grand Canyon's geological history: the eons of time during which rock strata were formed from sea floors, sand dunes, river beds, and volcanic material; the massive uplift of the Colorado Plateau; and the more recent period during which the Colorado River has been cutting down more than a mile through rock layers, exposing them as horizontal bands of countless colors on the canyon walls. In addition, weathering including cycles of freezing and thawing, has worn away at the walls, enlarging the canyon up to 18 miles at its greatest width.

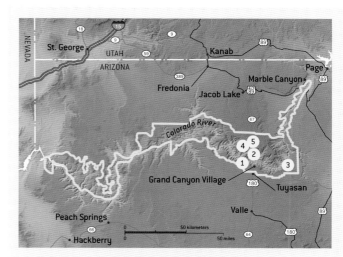

GRAND CANYON ARIZONA

AREA
1,218,375 acres (4,931 sq km)
ESTABLISHED
February 1919
VISITOR INFORMATION
(928) 638 7888;
www.nps.gov/grca

KEY ATTRACTIONS ① Hermit Road ② Rim Trail ③ Desert View Drive ④ Bright Angel Trail ⑤ Bright Angel Point
NOTABLE WILDLIFE California condor, mule deer, elk, black bear, mountain lion, tassel-eared squirrel

The pointed summit of Isis Temple rises dramatically on the north side of the Colorado River, surrounded by rugged, multicolored rocks of the Grand Canyon's walls and buttes. In the foreground runs a part of the Bright Angel Trail, the most popular route from the South Rim descending into the inner canyon.

The moon rises over the skeleton of a juniper in Grand Canyon's Horseshoe Mesa area. Reached by a 3-mile (one-way) trail beginning at Grandview Point, Horseshoe Mesa makes a rewarding day hike. Descending more than 2,500 feet, the route is not recommended for summer hikes because of lack of shade.

Once one of the world's most critically endangered species, the magnificent California condor has been the focus of intense conservation efforts. Visitors to the Grand Canyon may see birds from a reintroduced population, wearing numbered wing tags to help biologists keep track of individuals.

The Colorado River gorge near Nankoweap is known as Marble Canyon. Nearly 40 rock layers within Grand Canyon National Park have been identified by geologists, providing a virtual textbook of the history of the Earth dating back 1.7 billion years.

The national park receives around 5 million visitors a year, and the Grand Canyon Village area with its hotels, visitor centers, and other attractions can be crowded, especially in summer. One way to escape is to take the free shuttle bus along the 7-mile Hermit Road, which follows the South Rim west from Grand Canyon Village. The road provides access to some of the most breathtaking views in the park, including Hopi Point, one of the best places to watch sunset turn the canyon red-gold, and Pima Point, where on a quiet day the Colorado River can be heard rushing through Granite Rapid far below.

An even better idea is to hike part or all of the 12-mile Rim Trail, a generally flat and easy walk that follows the South Rim both east and west of Grand Canyon Village. Using the shuttle bus, it is possible to make a one-way hike and then return to the start without retracing your steps. Many visitors hike at least part-way down into the canyon, with the Bright Angel and South Kaibab Trails the most popular routes. Both trails offer fantastic views of rugged canyon walls and distant formations, though hikers should be aware of the difficulties of hiking back up to the rim after descending. The park's famed mule rides, following the Bright Angel Trail, provide a way to see part of the inner canyon without hiking.

The Desert View Drive follows the South Rim eastward for 26 miles, with views down to the Colorado River at Moran Point and Lipan Point, among other overlooks. The drive passes the historic Desert View Watchtower, built in 1932. The 70-foot-tall rock structure provides a fabulous panorama that takes in the Painted Desert to the east and the San Francisco Peaks to the south, as well as a broad swath of the Grand Canyon.

Only 10 percent of park visitors make their way to the North Rim of the canyon, 220 miles by road from the South Rim. Vistas here are no less spectacular than South Rim views, and overlooks are far less crowded. A half-mile trail leads from Grand Canyon Lodge to Bright Angel Point for an incredible panorama, including views into Bright Angel Canyon. A separate drive leads to Point Imperial, the highest point on the North Rim, and a close view of Mount Hayden with its rock spire. The road continues to Cape Royal, with views of Wotan's Throne, step-sided Vishnu Temple, and the eroded hole in a rock wall called Angel's Window. More than 1,000 feet higher than the South Rim, the North Rim is closed by heavy snow in winter.

Park rangers remind visitors to think of Grand Canyon National Park as three separate sections: the South Rim, the North Rim, and the Colorado River. The river flows through the park for 277 miles, and thousands of people each year enjoy running its whitewater rapids in rafts or boats. A river trip allows time for camping on the banks of the Colorado, as well as for seeing the Grand Canyon's mighty cliffs from a different perspective. Highly experienced boaters can take independent trips down the Colorado (permits are issued via lottery), but most visitors sign on with a commercial outfitter. River voyages can take two weeks or more, and for many participants the experience is the trip of a lifetime.

Whether from a rim viewpoint, a hiking trail, or a river raft, the awe-inspiring scenes of Grand Canyon National Park prove time and again the wisdom of President Theodore Roosevelt, who in 1903 asked the people of the United States never "to mar the wonderful grandeur, the sublimity, the great loneliness and beauty" of the canyon. "Leave it as it is," he said. "You cannot improve on it."

PETRIFIED FOREST NATIONAL PARK

THE BEAUTY OF PETRIFIED FOREST National Park is revealed in many ways, from the landscape scale to the miniature. On the broadest level is an expansive swath of terrain displaying such vivid colors that early explorers called it "painted"—a word that has endured through the years as an apt description of this desert region of northeastern Arizona. At the other end of the scale are fragments of fossilized wood, glittering in the sun like polished jewels in countless colors. In between, of course, are the huge petrified logs that led to this area's federal protection as a national monument in 1906.

The park preserves what may be the largest concentration of petrified wood in the world. The logs here began their existence more than 220 million years ago as trees up to 200 feet tall, growing in what was then a hot, humid environment. Many were coniferous trees of a type that may be related to modern monkey puzzle trees and Norfolk Island pines.

These trees died, fell to the ground, and were probably transported by rivers, piling up in log jams where they were then buried under mud and sand. The mineral silica, of volcanic origin, replaced the trees' organic matter and was transformed into crystalline quartz. The quartz is mixed with smaller amounts of iron, manganese, and carbon, which provide the logs' brilliant spectrum of colors. Conditions of burial, moisture, and mineralization had to coincide for the array of petrified logs to exist, lying buried for millions of years until erosion of this part of the Colorado Plateau exposed them on the Earth's surface.

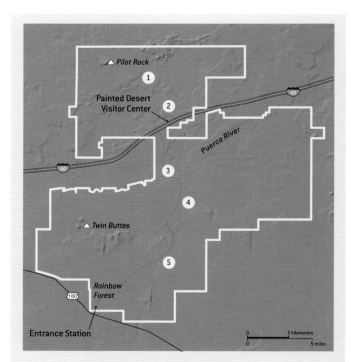

PETRIFIED FOREST ARIZONA

AREA
93,533 acres (379 sq km)
ESTABLISHED
December 1962
VISITOR INFORMATION
(928) 524 6228;
www.nps.gov/pefo

KEY ATTRACTIONS ① Painted Desert ② Painted Desert Inn ③ Puerco Pueblo ④ Blue Mesa ⑤ Crystal Forest
NOTABLE WILDLIFE Pronghorn, mule deer, badger, swift fox, Gunnison's prairie dog

A 28-mile scenic drive traverses the park and provides access to the best of its landscape features and to aggregations of petrified logs, as well as to Native American archeological sites. Most visitors enter the park from Interstate 40, stopping at the Painted Desert Visitor Center to see exhibits including information on the many fossils collected from the park. More than just giant logs are preserved here: Scientists have found fossils of early dinosaur-like reptiles related to modern crocodiles, among many other species of animals and plants.

Heading north and then looping back southward, the scenic drive passes several viewpoints overlooking the region called the Painted Desert. The fantastic assemblage of badlands scenery here—mesas, buttes, cliffs, and ravines—displays strata of sandstone, mudstone, limestone, ash, and other material, showing colors from blue to buff to reddish depending on the minerals they contain. The hues of the Painted Desert are most vivid near sunrise or sunset, especially after rain.

Entering the southern portion of the park, the drive reaches Puerco Pueblo, the remains of a community of the Ancestral Puebloan culture, occupied in the 13th and 14th centuries. The village of around 200 people occupied more than 100 rooms constructed of sandstone blocks, and grew crops of corn, beans, and squash. A short trail winds among the remains of dwellings, passing by many petroglyphs (figures incised in rock), including some with astronomical significance.

A side road leads to the spectacular landscape of Blue Mesa, with conical hills and ridges of bentonite, a clay formed from volcanic ash. One predominant color of Blue Mesa is indeed bluish, but some strata show shades of purple, red, and gray. The properties of bentonite, in particular its extreme instability when wet, make it inhospitable to vegetation.

Some petrified wood can be found at Blue Mesa, but the highest concentrations are found to the south, at sites such as Crystal Forest, where a 0.75-mile trail winds through an area of fossil log sections containing beautiful crystals. Many of these crystals were taken by collectors before the park was established, and some continue to be removed illegally by modern visitors.

Sedimentary strata dating back millions of years give formations in the Painted Desert their "layer cake" appearance. Though red predominates in this photograph, colors can range from pale buff to yellow to purplish, depending on the minerals found in rocks. Dawn or dusk light creates the most vivid vistas.

Long, powerful front claws enable badgers to excavate the burrows where they sleep and raise young, as well as to dig out the rodents, including prairie dogs, on which they prey. Badger tunnels have several entrances, each with a pile of dirt nearby. Badgers are members of the weasel family.

A 0.4-mile trail at the Giant Logs area leads to some of the most impressive and colorfully decorated petrified trees in the national park. One log, named "Old Faithful," is almost 10 feet in diameter. An even larger concentration of petrified wood lies along the 1.6-mile Long Logs Trail, where it is believed that a great number of dead trees piled up in a massive log jam after being carried down a river from their original location. Here, as elsewhere in the park, the petrified wood displays an amazing clarity of detail: grain, rings, knotholes, and other once-living features are reproduced in exactitude by crystalline quartz in stunningly beautiful colors. (It is for good reason that one part of the park is called Rainbow Forest.) Because bark quickly falls from dead trees, it is rarely found fossilized in the area, although the park museum displays some examples.

Petrified logs in the park are broken so cleanly that some visitors imagine they must have been cut by a saw—the ends of the logs seem unnaturally even and smooth. The sharpness of the breaks, however, is a result of the internal structure of quartz. Some logs in the park were originally close to 200 feet in length, and are thought to have been broken into smaller sections during the period of geological uplift of the Colorado Plateau.

The Ancestral Puebloans used petrified wood for tools such as knives and scrapers. Agate House, a small structure near the Long Logs Trail, demonstrates another use of petrified wood: as building blocks of an eight-room pueblo thought to have been occupied about 700 years ago.

Just north of the national park's southern boundary, the Rainbow Forest Museum offers regular ranger-led walks along the Giant Logs Trail, during which interpreters discuss many aspects of the park, including how petrified wood formed and the kinds of fossils found in the area.

Collared lizards prefer habitats with boulders on which they can bask for warmth and scan for prey. In Petrified Forest National Park, petrified logs serve the same purpose. In some regions the collared lizard has mysteriously acquired the folk name "mountain boomer," though it makes no sound.

The long legs of burrowing owls are an adaptation to a life spent mostly on the ground and inside tunnels. This species is commonly found in association with prairie dogs, sharing the burrows dug by the small rodents. This individual wears a leg band placed by a biologist for scientific research.

SAGUARO NATIONAL PARK

FEW AMERICAN LANDSCAPES ARE AS dramatic as the spectacle of thousands of saguaro cacti arrayed across the foothills of southern Arizona—an otherworldly forest of green giants, simultaneously massive and spindly, towering over the surrounding vegetation. And no scene is more emblematic of its geographic location, because *Carnegiea gigantea* grows nowhere else on Earth but the Sonoran Desert ecoregion of the southwestern United States and adjacent Mexico.

Saguaro National Park encompasses 137 square miles in two separate units, one east and one west of the city of Tucson. The park is best known for its desert habitat, home to giant saguaros, and it is here that most visitors spend their time. Yet the park hosts much more than cacti. Peaks in the eastern Rincon Mountain District rise to an elevation of 8,666 feet, an environment where black bears and white-tailed deer roam through forests of ponderosa pine, oak, and Douglas-fir. Saguaro National Park also offers fine opportunities for hiking, biking,

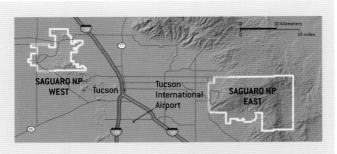

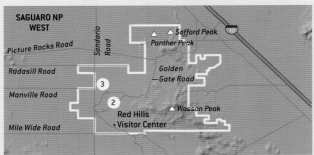

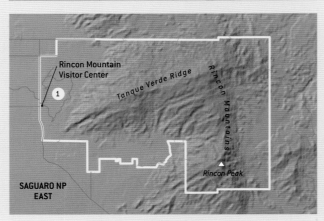

SAGUARO ARIZONA

AREA
87,526 acres (354 sq km)
ESTABLISHED
October 1994
VISITOR INFORMATION
(520) 733 5153;
www.nps.gov/sagu

KEY ATTRACTIONS ① Cactus Forest Drive ② Bajada Loop Drive ③ Petroglyphs
NOTABLE WILDLIFE Black bear, mountain lion, mule deer, collared peccary, desert tortoise, Gila monster, greater roadrunner

horseback riding, and wilderness camping, and preserves a significant collection of Native American petroglyphs (rock carvings).

Many travelers get their first experience of the park on the Rincon Mountain District's 8-mile Cactus Forest Drive, a loop through an expanse of giant saguaros. The drive features viewpoints with superb vistas of the Sonoran Desert. Much of the loop is one-way, with the route meandering across desert washes and over hills.

Several trails are located along the Cactus Forest Drive, including the short, easy Desert Ecology Trail, with interpretive signs introducing many local plants and animals. The Freeman Homestead Trail leads a half-mile to a pioneer homestead, passing through a grove of large, mature saguaros where walkers can examine these amazing plants closely.

Soaring up to 50 feet high, with its distinctive multi-armed shape, the giant saguaro can live to be 200 years old and may weigh as much as 6 tons. Yet these goliaths of the desert begin their lives as tiny, extremely vulnerable seedlings whose existence can be ended by a single human footstep. An eight-year-old saguaro may be less than 2 inches tall. Many start growing in the shelter of a "nurse tree" such as a palo verde, later rising high above it.

Saguaros begin producing their large, beautiful white flowers when about 35 years old. Bats feed on the flower nectar and pollinate saguaros, which then produce fruits that provide food for birds, mammals, reptiles, and insects. Gila woodpeckers often excavate nest cavities in saguaro trunks. The pleated trunks of saguaros allow them to soak up massive amounts of water during desert rains, expanding their girth dramatically.

Adventurous hikers can use the Tanque Verde Ridge Trail to enter the Rincon Mountains, which rise to the east of the Cactus Forest Drive. A sign indicates the parking area for the trailhead along the drive. Nearly 58,000 acres of the park are included in a designated wilderness area, with six campgrounds located at elevations up to 8,000 feet. The woodland environment here is far different than that of the desert below. The lush forests of the Rincons receive more precipitation than the surrounding lowlands. White trunks of aspens are scattered among conifers and oaks, reminiscent of mountains much farther north.

The Tucson Mountain District of the national park is located 30 miles west of the Rincon Mountain District, on the opposite side of Tucson. Here, the 6-mile Bajada Loop Drive offers panoramas of some of the most densely growing stands of saguaros in the park. One of the highlights of the drive is the Valley View Overlook Trail, which passes through desert washes to ascend a ridge with wonderful views of the Avra Valley and distinctively pointed Picacho Peak in the distance.

North of the scenic drive, the Signal Hill Petroglyph Trail passes dozens of examples of Native American rock art along a half-mile route. Images include human figures, animals, and geometric designs whose meanings are mysterious, though some may have astronomical significance. The petroglyphs were created by people of the Hohokam culture around 1,700 to 600 years ago. An audiovisual

Visitors to the Tucson Mountain District can observe Native American petroglyphs, or figures incised into rocks (often called "desert varnish"). Abstract designs and representational figures are included among the park's petroglyphs, some of which may have been used for astronomical observation.

The only poisonous lizard in the United States, the Gila monster can grow to 14 inches in length. Not aggressive unless handled or provoked, this desert-dwelling reptile poses little threat to humans. Its shiny, brightly colored scales give the Gila monster's skin the appearance of beautifully designed beadwork.

presentation at the Red Hills Visitor Center provides a Native American perspective on the giant saguaro cactus and the Sonoran Desert.

Several other trails provide plenty of hiking opportunities in the Tucson Mountain District, including routes that ascend Wasson Peak, at 4,687 feet the highest point in the Tucson Mountains. Vistas from this and other lookouts take in a breathtaking expanse of saguaros, growing among scattered outcrops of rocky hills. Geologists have called the complicated and jumbled-together rocks here the "Tucson Mountain Chaos." One theory holds that these uplands slid here from the top of the Santa Catalina Mountains far to the east—but regardless of their origin, they contribute to a strikingly attractive landscape.

While the giant saguaro reigns as the star of the park's natural world, the Sonoran Desert is home to a fascinating array of wildlife, as well. The greater roadrunner is everyone's favorite bird, sprinting across the ground in search of lizards and other prey. Collared peccaries, the pig-like mammals also known as javelinas, roam the desert washes in family groups of a dozen or more. The spiny little reptiles known as horned lizards are seen frequently in the park, and are often incorrectly called "horned toads" by visitors. The popular name come from the lizard's rounded body and blunt snout, which make it resemble a toad.

Although the giant saguaro deserves its place as an iconic symbol of the Southwest, visitors who stop to enjoy the sight of a grove of these cacti have only begun their exploration of Saguaro National Park.

The black-tailed rattlesnake is one of six species of rattlers found in Saguaro National Park. Among the others are the Mojave rattlesnake, known for its highly toxic venom, and the sidewinder, which travels with a curious sideways motion. Most snakes in the park are active at night, when temperatures are more moderate.

JOSHUA TREE NATIONAL PARK

The many-armed yuccas that gave Joshua Tree National Park its name are among the distinctive plants of the Mojave Desert. Here they grow among large boulders of monzogranite, landscape features that have made the park one of the country's most popular destinations for serious rock climbers.

JOSHUA TREE NATIONAL PARK RANKS WITH America's best places to appreciate the beauty and diversity of a desert environment: the elemental landscape of rock, sand, and sky; the many ways life has adapted to a demanding climate; the unexpected lushness of an oasis; the spectacular burst of colors when spring wildflowers bloom.

Encompassing two desert ecosystems and countless vistas of strikingly attractive scenery, Joshua Tree appeals to a range of travelers. Park Boulevard, the national park's scenic drive, offers rewarding sightseeing for those who have limited time. Yet nearly three-fourths of the park's 1,240 square miles has been designated as wilderness, providing unlimited adventure for backcountry hikers. Rock-climbers, history buffs, and nature-lovers all find special enjoyment at Joshua Tree, as well.

The park is named for the Joshua tree, a yucca (in the lily family) that grows to 40 feet high or more. The tree's silhouette is the iconic image of the park, with twisting branches ending in bundles of pointed leaves. Native Americans used the plant's seeds for food and its leaves for baskets and sandals. Its English name is said to come from early Mormon settlers, who believed the tree's limbs looked like the upraised arms of the Biblical Joshua, urging them to continue their journey. Stalks of cream-white flowers on Joshua trees are one of the first signs of spring in the park.

Biologists know Joshua Tree National Park as the meeting place of two major desert ecosystems. The eastern section of the park, generally below 3,000 feet in elevation, comprises part of the Colorado Desert, itself a part of the larger Sonoran Desert. The western, higher part of the park lies within the Mojave Desert. Even non-scientists can easily see and appreciate the differences in the two habitats.

Notably hotter and drier than the Mojave Desert, the Colorado Desert is typified by vegetation such as creosote bush, ocotillo, and cholla cactus. The pungent smell of creosote bush, filling the air after summer rains, is an instantly recognizable aspect of southwestern deserts. The Mojave Desert of the western

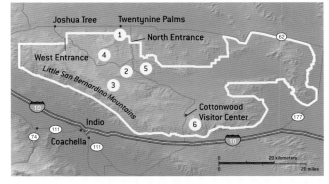

JOSHUA TREE CALIFORNIA

AREA
770,984 acres (3,120 sq km)

ESTABLISHED
October 1994

VISITOR INFORMATION
(760) 367 5500;
www.nps.gov/jotr

KEY ATTRACTIONS ① Oasis of
Mara ② Skull Rock ③ Keys View
④ Hidden Valley ⑤ Arch Rock
⑥ Mastodon Peak

NOTABLE WILDLIFE Bighorn
sheep, coyote, kit fox, mule deer,
mountain lion, desert tortoise

The monzogranite of Joshua Tree National Park erodes into a wide array of odd shapes, providing endless opportunity and challenge for rock climbers, as well as striking scenery for other visitors. Here in the park's Jumbo Rocks area, a sphere balances in a weathered crack in the rocks.

During most of their lives, ocotillos appear to be nearly lifeless bundles of scrawny, whip-like limbs. When rains come to the desert, though, they quickly sprout green leaves all along their branches. The bright red flowers appear annually, providing the reason for the scientific name splendens.

One of the most distinctive landscape features in the park is the aptly named Skull Rock, a monzogranite boulder that seems to display eye and nose cavities. A 1.7-mile nature trail winds past Skull Rock, offering a lesson in park geology and a chance to observe Mojave Desert flora and fauna.

park receives more precipitation, and can be most obviously identified by the presence of Joshua trees, which do not grow in the Colorado Desert.

Travelers who enter the park via the Oasis Visitor Center in the town of Twentynine Palms can easily get acquainted with another of the area's habitats—this one perhaps the most attractive of all. The Oasis of Mara is one of five fan palm oases in the park, spots where water comes to the surface along underground fault lines, creating a green haven for life in the dry desert. Growing here are splendid examples of the desert fan palm, which can be up to 75 feet tall. Its large green leaves are named for their pleated fan shape. A distinctive "petticoat" of dead leaves hangs down along the tree's trunk. Native Americans of the Serrano culture lived at this site hundreds of years ago, cultivating crops such as beans and squash. Today, a half-mile nature trail allows visitors to enjoy the verdant oasis and the variety of birds that make it their home.

Park Boulevard runs westward into the Mojave Desert through one of the national park's most famous and popular features, a bizarre landscape of huge boulders of a magma-born rock called monzogranite. Perfect for rock-climbing, these boulders have been traced with more than 8,000 climbing routes. Erosion has worked on the monzogranite for millennia, creating fantastic shapes and rock jumbles. Much can be seen from Park Boulevard, and the 1.7-mile Skull Rock Nature Trail allows hikers to wind through this striking terrain, viewing a rock with two eroded "eye sockets" and a domed crown.

Passing extensive stands of Joshua trees, Park Boulevard reaches the side road to Keys View, a high lookout point on a ridge of the Little San Bernardino Mountains. The tremendous panorama to the south takes in the Coachella Valley far below—including the famed San Andreas Fault, which has caused so many violent Californian earthquakes—and mountains including 11,500-foot San Gorgonio Mountain, often capped with snow. On a clear day, views extend past the Salton Sea and south into Mexico.

At a site to the north of Park Boulevard, park rangers lead guided tours of Keys Ranch, where a family lived for 50 years, surviving in the desert by mining and farming. Household items, equipment, and ranch buildings illustrate the hardscrabble life of a couple and their five children in this remote and seemingly inhospitable canyon, from 1917 to 1969. A nearby side road leads to a trail through Hidden Valley. One of the finest scenic areas in the park, this intimate canyon is nearly surrounded by tall walls of granite. It is rumored that old-time cattle rustlers hid their stolen livestock in this spot.

Wilson Canyon Road leads through the eastern part of Joshua Tree National Park, between the Pinto and Hexie Mountains, into Pinto Basin, and then south to the park's southern entrance station. On the way it passes the nature trail to Arch Rock, a graceful formation of pinkish granite. The road traverses the Colorado Desert, and a short trail at Cholla Cactus Garden identifies some of the plants of the area, including the oddly jointed cactus called cholla. Vast spaces are covered in creosote bush, where thousands of plants grow evenly spaced from each other. Chemicals emitted into the soil discourage adjacent growth and lessen competition for scarce rainfall.

Visitors with high-clearance vehicles, as well as mountain bikers, can enjoy an expansive network of backcountry roads through the park, taking travelers far away from developed areas. One such opportunity is the 18-mile Geology Tour Road, heading south off Park Boulevard. A brochure is available explaining the origins of the surrounding terrain, including some of the most impressive granite formations in the park. The road passes old mining sites on its way to a dam built by early ranchers to provide water for their cattle.

CHANNEL ISLANDS NATIONAL PARK

AN ASTOUNDING ARRAY OF NATURAL beauty is encompassed in the relatively small land area of Channel Islands National Park: rugged seacoasts battered by crashing waves; striking rock formations including what may be the world's largest sea cave; lonely beaches; grasslands bright with wildflowers; and hillsides of globally rare Mediterranean-type chaparral vegetation.

Even more spectacular sights can be found in the sea around these five islands off the coast of southern California, and in the air over them. Whales, dolphins, seals, and sea lions swim in Pacific Ocean waters, and the islands host the largest breeding colonies of seabirds in the region. So many rare and endemic species are found here that the Channel Islands have been called "the Galapagos of North America."

The Channel Islands can be reached only by boat or airplane, which means that, despite their beauty and natural appeal, this is among the least visited of the national parks. The park has two visitor centers on the mainland, in the cities of Santa Barbara and Ventura. Concessioners offer a variety of boat trips to explore the islands, beginning with half-day cruises that circle islands for views of rocky cliffs, marine mammals, and birds. Visitors with more time can land on one of the islands and camp, transport a sea kayak to an island to paddle along the shore, or bring snorkeling or diving gear. Other day cruises are offered seasonally to see several species of whales, which congregate in the Pacific around the islands.

Santa Cruz is the largest of the islands at 96 square miles, and is jointly owned by the National Park Service and the Nature Conservancy. With mountain summits rising above 2,000 feet, it features the most diverse environment of any of the five national park islands. On the northwestern coast is Painted Cave, a vast sea cave almost a quarter-mile long, with an entrance 160 feet high. Along with its breeding seals and sea lions, Santa Cruz is home to an endemic bird called the island scrub-jay, much sought-after by visiting birdwatchers.

The thickest fur of any animal made the sea otter a prized catch for hunters, and brought this marine member of the weasel family to the brink of extinction. Restoration efforts including reintroductions have brought sea otters back to areas of the California coast where they once thrived.

PACIFIC OCEAN

CHANNEL ISLANDS CALIFORNIA

AREA
249,561 acres (1,010 sq km)

ESTABLISHED
March 1980

VISITOR INFORMATION
(805) 658 5730;
www.nps.gov/chis

KEY ATTRACTIONS
① Painted Cave ② Arch Rock

NOTABLE WILDLIFE Elephant seal, California sea lion, northern fur seal, harbor seal, island fox, island scrub-jay, gray whale, blue whale

Waves break on rocks at Chinese
Beach, on Santa Cruz Island.
California's largest island, Santa
Cruz encompasses 96 square miles
and the highest mountain in the
national park: 2,450-foot Diablo
Peak. Santa Cruz serves as the only
home for the island scrub-jay, a
colorful member of the crow family.

*California sea lions bask
atop beach rocks on San
Miguel Island, where
thousands of pinnipeds
(seals and sea lions) gather
to breed each year. Other
species found in the park
include Guadalupe fur
seals, Steller's sea lions,
northern fur seals,
northern elephant seals,
and harbor seals.*

The westernmost island, San Miguel, is best known for hosting
up to five species of seals and sea lions, with awesome
gatherings of up to 30,000 individuals. Santa Rosa, the second-
largest island, offers white sand beaches and a significant
number of rare plants, including a subspecies of the very rare
Torrey pine. The smallest of the islands, Santa Barbara,
encompasses only 1 square mile, but provides habitat for
breeding seals and sea lions and the largest known nesting
colony of a rare seabird called Xantus's murrelet.

Spectacular Anacapa Island (which actually comprises several
small islets) features strikingly rugged sea cliffs and caves, as
well as 40-foot-high Arch Rock, a wave-cut natural bridge.
Thousands of birds nest on its various islands. In summer, park
rangers take video cameras and microphones on dives into the
Pacific Ocean kelp forests around the island, allowing visitors to
observe sea life from dry land.

Other wildlife species on the islands include the once
endangered bald eagle and peregrine falcon, predatory birds
that are making a comeback after decades of declining
population, and the beautiful island fox, no bigger than a house
cat. There are six subspecies of the island fox, each unique to
the Channel Island on which it lives.

DEATH VALLEY NATIONAL PARK

SIMPLE STATISTICS TELL PART OF THE STORY of Death Valley National Park. It is known as the lowest place in North America (282 feet below sea level) and notorious as the hottest and driest place on the continent. These superlatives alone attract many visitors, eager to experience a land of such extremes.

But there is more to Death Valley than numbers, no matter how compelling. Geological forces have created landscapes of truly bizarre shapes within the park, which also encompasses sand dunes, rugged canyons, and badlands spires, with snow-capped mountains looming more than 11,000 feet overhead. Adding to the park's appeal are historic sites from the pioneer era and a "castle" with an odd and intriguing past.

The best introduction to the park is the Furnace Creek area, which includes a visitor center, orientation program, and the Death Valley Museum, with exhibits on the area's natural and human history. It was here in July, 1913, that the temperature reached 134°F (57°C), the second-highest figure ever recorded on Earth. The summer of 1996 saw 40 days with the temperature topping 120°F (49°C). Rainfall in Death Valley averages less than 2 inches a year.

A number of factors contribute to the park's extreme climate, including its terrain of a long, narrow valley below sea level surrounded by mountains that trap heat. Mountain ranges to the west intercept moisture-carrying clouds, creating a "rain shadow" over the park. There have been years when no rain at all fell in Death Valley.

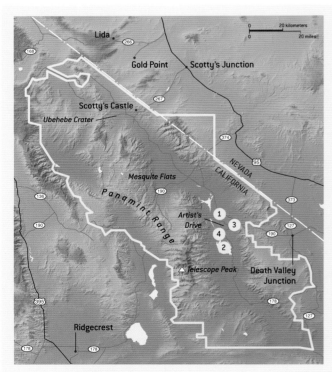

DEATH VALLEY CALIFORNIA, NEVADA

AREA
3,373,041 acres (13,650 sq km)

ESTABLISHED
October 1994

VISITOR INFORMATION
(760) 786 3200;
www.nps.gov/deva

KEY ATTRACTIONS ① Furnace Creek ② Badwater Basin ③ Zabriskie Point ④ Devil's Golf Course

NOTABLE WILDLIFE Bighorn sheep, coyote, mountain lion, kit fox, desert tortoise, greater roadrunner

Lying in a depression 282 feet below sea level, Death Valley's Badwater Basin is famed as the lowest point in North America. Salt flats here cover almost 200 square miles, creating an environment too extreme for nearly all plants and animals. A temporary lake may form on the flats after rains.

Visitors can stand at the lowest place in North America by driving to Badwater Basin, 17 miles south of Furnace Creek. Here, covering nearly 200 square miles, is an otherworldly landscape of barren, gleaming-white salt flats, a natural habitat inhospitable to almost all forms of life. Occasional floods in distant mountains drain to this flat expanse, creating a temporary lake that quickly evaporates in the heat, leaving behind a crust of mineral salts.

Other destinations near Furnace Creek include an interpretive hiking trail into aptly named Golden Canyon, where picturesquely eroded walls show especially vivid golden color at sunset. Artist's Drive is a 9-mile loop road through a terrain of multicolored rocks, some of volcanic origin, displaying hues from buff to greenish and pink. The Devil's Golf Course is a large tract of rock salt pushed up into spires and eroded into countless jagged shapes.

The park's most famous spot for enjoying the landscape colors of sunrise is Zabriskie Point, along the highway to the southeast of Furnace Creek. The vista here takes in waves of weirdly eroded badland ridges in yellow and brown, with Death Valley's Badwater Basin in the distance and the Panamint Range of mountains on the horizon. Telescope Peak is the high point of the Panamints at 11,049 feet, making an elevation difference of more than 2 miles from Badwater Basin only 12 miles to the east.

Just south of Zabriskie Point is Twenty Mule Team Canyon, named for the animals that hauled wagons weighing more than 35 tons during Death Valley's borax-mining era of the late 19th century. Here a 2.7-mile drive loops through some of the park's most striking badlands terrain. North of Furnace Creek, the Harmony Borax Works preserves the site of a borax refinery, which in the 1880s produced the mineral salt used for soap-making and industrial purposes.

The national park's Stovepipe Wells area is noted for the expansive Mesquite Flat sand dunes, some of which rise to heights of almost 100 feet. Photographers visit this area at various times of the day to capture the way the light accents sensuous dune shapes. At nearby Mosaic Canyon, a quarter-mile trail leads into a narrow ravine with walls of smooth, water-sculpted marble.

Every visitor to Death Valley National Park should see the amazing house named Death Valley Ranch, more commonly known as Scotty's Castle. The story behind this fancifully turreted Spanish-Mediterranean mansion seems stranger than fiction: A shady gold prospector named Walter Scott spent years telling visitors that he had constructed his "castle" with riches from his mines. In fact, it had been built in the 1920s as a vacation home by a wealthy businessman, Albert Johnson, who had been an investor in Scott's nonexistent gold mines. Despite Scott's fraudulent scheming, the two men became lifelong friends, and Johnson later allowed Scott to live in the never finished house. Park rangers lead daily tours of Scotty's Castle.

Ubehebe Crater, one the park's most amazing sights, is located 8 miles west of Scotty's Castle. Just a few centuries ago—a single heartbeat in geological time—hot magma rising up through the Earth's crust reached a pocket of groundwater, turning it to steam. The result was a massive explosion that

The Devil's Golf Course area is known for fantastically eroded formations of rock salt, shaped by rain and wind into a devilishly forbidding terrain. Like the Badwater Basin flats, this site is covered in salt concentrated by a basin where water evaporates, rather than drains away in an outlet river.

Many visitors picture Death Valley as a place of endless sandy desert, yet less than 1 percent of the national park is covered in sand dunes. For dunes to form, there must be a source of sand (such as desert washes), winds to carry the sand, and terrain that "traps" wind-blown sand in a particular location.

created a crater 600 feet deep and a half-mile across. Several similar features, called maar volcanos, are nearby, but Ubehebe is the youngest and largest. Cinders still lie as much as 150 feet deep around the crater rim. The red-and-gray walls of the massive crater compose a colorful scene that gives little hint of its violent birth.

Away from the main routes, miles of primitive backcountry roads are available to visitors with high-clearance four-wheel-drive vehicles, including Racetrack Road, which leads south from Ubehebe Crater to a mysterious site called the Racetrack. In a dry lake bed here, rocks move across the Earth, leaving long tracks behind, for reasons still debated by scientists. Although no one has actually seen the rocks move, it is believed that wet, slippery soil after rain allows high winds to push them along.

Death Valley's more than 1,000 miles of paved and dirt roads (more than any other national park) allow exploration of remote areas, but drivers should plan carefully before setting out. Many roads see little traffic, and a breakdown in summer could be dangerous without adequate water. Help could be a long walk away.

Death Valley Ranch, a Spanish Mediterranean-style mansion, creates a bizarre vision in the Grapevine Canyon area. Begun by a wealthy couple in the 1920s but never finished, the house is also known as Scotty's Castle, for an eccentric local prospector named Walter Scott who claimed to own it.

SEQUOIA NATIONAL PARK

UNDERSTANDABLY, MOST VISITORS ARRIVE at Sequoia National Park with one goal foremost in mind: to see the largest living things on Earth. Here, and in adjacent Kings Canyon National Park to the north, grow expansive groves of awe-inspiring giant sequoia trees, which in their millennia-long lives can reach 300 feet in height with a circumference of well over 100 feet.

Although not as tall as their cousins the coast redwoods of northern California, the giant sequoias of the Sierra Nevadas have a greater overall volume, thanks to their massive girth. The famed General Sherman Tree of Sequoia National Park is more than 36 feet in diameter at its base, with a volume of more than 52,000 cubic feet, and is widely accepted as the world's largest tree.

While the simple act of standing nearby to admire these ancient giants justifies a trip to Sequoia, the park offers much more to see and do, encompassing a notable diversity of environment and wildlife. Elevations in the park range from oak chaparral forest at 1,300 feet to the treeless alpine summit of Mount Whitney, which at 14,505 feet is the highest point in the United States outside Alaska. Craggy mountain peaks, lush meadows, beautiful rivers, glacier-carved canyons, and a marble cave beckon visitors to explore Sequoia National Park beyond the legendary groves of *Sequoiadendron giganteum*.

Travelers reaching the park at the Ash Meadows Entrance, close to the Foothills Visitor Center, follow Generals Highway along the Middle Fork of the Kaweah River. At Hospital Rock, exhibits focus on the Native Americans who once lived here; nearby are pictographs and hollows in rock once used for grinding acorns into flour for food.

Leaving the riverside, the road climbs in dizzying curves into coniferous forest of white fir, ponderosa and sugar pines, and

Found only in the Sierra Nevadas of California, the giant sequoia ranks as Earth's largest tree species by volume. Mature individuals can have a circumference of more than 100 feet, and add about 40 cubic feet of wood annually as new growth. Some of the trees in the national park are believed to be between 1,800 and 2,700 years old.

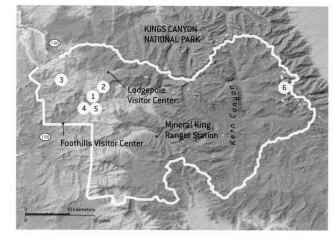

SEQUOIA CALIFORNIA

AREA
403,890 acres (1,634 sq km)
ESTABLISHED
October 1890
VISITOR INFORMATION
(559) 565 3341;
www.nps.gov/seki

KEY ATTRACTIONS ① Giant Forest
② General Sherman Tree
③ Crystal Cave ④ Moro Rock
⑤ Tunnel Log ⑥ Mount Whitney
NOTABLE WILDLIFE Black bear,
mountain lion, mule deer, bighorn
sheep, yellow-bellied marmot, pika

The highest mountain in the United States outside Alaska, 14,494-foot Mount Whitney rises on the eastern boundary of Sequoia National Park. The peak's popularity as a destination for mountain climbers has led to a permit system aimed at minimizing environmental damage.

Black bears, such as this cub, may be encountered nearly anywhere in Sequoia National Park. Feeding mostly on plant material such as roots, berries, and nuts, as well as insects, bears have an acute sense of smell and can be attracted to odors of cooking or cached food.

giant sequoia. The lookout at Amphitheater Point offers far-reaching views over canyons and ridges; to the northeast rises the granite dome of Moro Rock.

A side road (accessible in summer only) leads to Crystal Cave, the only one of more than 200 caves in Sequoia and Kings Canyon open for guided tours. Tickets for the tours are sold at either the Foothills or Lodgepole Visitor Centers, not at the cave itself. A marble cave, rather than the more common limestone, Crystal has more than 3 miles of passages featuring superb speleothems (cave formations) including some rare varieties.

Ahead lies the heart of the park, the Giant Forest, with its groves of giant sequoias. The Giant Forest Museum is a good first stop, to learn about the life cycle of these trees and what the park does to protect them and promote seedling growth. In recent years the park has been conducting prescribed burns in sequoia groves, the result of discoveries about the importance of fire in maintaining healthy forests. The 0.7-mile Big Trees Trail here circles Round Meadow, with signs providing more information about sequoias.

Nearby, a side road leads to the trail to the top of 6,725-foot Moro Rock, which rewards a fairly strenuous climb (up 400 stairsteps) with panoramic views over the Sierra Nevada

foothills; visibility can be 100 miles on a clear day. The road also leads to the park's famous Tunnel Log, a giant sequoia that fell in 1937. A tunnel 17 feet wide and 8 feet high was cut through the trunk, allowing vehicles of standard size to pass through.

The park's star attraction, the General Sherman Tree, is reached via a trail off a side road north of the Giant Forest Museum. Visitors who have taken time to admire this incredible sight can then follow the Congress Trail, a 2-mile loop hike through the sequoia grove, for a more intense immersion in the world of these unique trees.

The side road to the Lodgepole Visitor Center turns east off the main park highway. A highlight here is the 1.7-mile Tokopah Trail, which follows the Marble Fork of the Kaweah River through a glacier-carved granite canyon, with the jagged 1,800-foot Watchtower formation looming overhead. The path ends at Tokopah Falls, which flows most impressively in early summer, a ribbon of whitewater down a rocky ravine.

Before Generals Highway reaches the park boundary, a side road leads to Dorst Campground and the trailhead for the 2.1-mile hike to the Muir Grove of giant sequoias, named for famed 19th-century Scottish-American conservationist John Muir. His activism led to the preservation not just of Sequoia National Park but also Yosemite Valley and other wilderness areas. Muir founded the Sierra Club, still one of the most important conservation organizations in the country. This walk is a fine escape from the crowds at other sequoia groves, with splendid stands of trees in a relatively isolated setting.

Sequoia National Park's Mineral King area is reached by a steep, winding road running up the East Fork of the Kaweah River, ending in a beautiful glacier-formed subalpine valley. Site of a historic mining community, Mineral King was once proposed for development as a ski resort before the area was added to the national park. Sharp-pointed Sawtooth Peak, 12,343 feet high, is the most prominent of the mountains ringing this picturesque valley. The easy, 1-mile Cold Springs Nature Trail provides a fine introduction to the area. The Monarch Lakes Trail ascends over 4.2 miles to Upper and Lower Monarch Lakes, at the base of Sawtooth Peak. Hikers willing to keep climbing another 1.3 miles will reach Sawtooth Pass, with one of the most spectacular views in the national park.

Mount Whitney, the highest mountain in the lower 48 states, lies on the eastern border of Sequoia National Park. Because of the topography of the Sierra Nevadas, however, it is not visible from any park roads. Climbing this peak from trailheads within the national park requires a permit and a multi-day backpacking trip. Permits are also required for all backcountry camping, and campers must use bear-resistant food-storage containers to prevent potentially dangerous encounters with black bears, which are common in the park. Hikers should know what to do if they encounter a bear on the trail, including attempting to scare it away by making a loud noise through clapping or yelling, and throwing objects at it from a safe distance. All sightings should be reported to a park ranger.

More than 270 feet tall, with a volume of 50,000 cubic feet, the General Sherman giant sequoia is the world's largest tree. Thick bark helps the species resist fire, disease, and insects, but fire suppression has led to poor growth of seedlings. New management techniques promote increased regeneration in the park.

KINGS CANYON NATIONAL PARK

KINGS CANYON NATIONAL PARK LIES adjacent to Sequoia National Park, contiguous with its northern border, and is administered jointly with its neighbor park. Like Sequoia, Kings Canyon protects magnificent groves of giant sequoia trees, the Earth's largest living things, and also offers visitors beautiful Sierra Nevada mountain scenery. The park is composed of two separate units. The great majority of its area has been designated as roadless wilderness, offering endless backcountry opportunity to hikers, backpackers, and horseback riders.

Kings Canyon's most popular site is Grant Grove, with a visitor center and amenities including lodging. Attention here centers on the 268-foot-tall General Grant Tree, the third-largest giant sequoia known (which makes it the world's third-largest living organism). The General Grant Tree is the only living thing to have been designated by the U.S. Congress as a national shrine, dedicated to those who have given their lives in service to their country. The half-mile trail here also passes the Fallen Monarch, a long-dead sequoia whose hollow interior is so big the U.S. Army once used it as a stable for 32 horses.

Nearby are possibilities for more extensive looks at giant sequoia groves. The 1.5-mile North Grove Loop Trail begins near the General Grant Tree and winds through meadows and forest where sequoias grow among other conifers. To the south, a rough, unpaved 2-mile road leads to Redwood Canyon, the world's largest grove of sequoias. Sixteen miles of loop trails here allow hikes from short strolls to overnight treks. Throughout the park, wilderness permits—obtained for free from visitor centers and self-service permit stations—are needed for overnight camping outside designated car campgrounds. No permits are needed for day hikes.

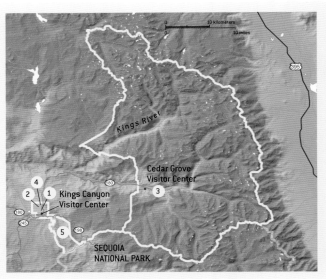

KINGS CANYON CALIFORNIA

AREA
461,846 acres (1,869 sq km)
ESTABLISHED
March 1940
VISITOR INFORMATION
(559) 565 3341;
www.nps.gov/seki

KEY ATTRACTIONS ① Grant Grove ② General Grant Tree ③ Kings Canyon ④ Panoramic Point Road ⑤ Redwood Canyon
NOTABLE WILDLIFE Black bear, mountain lion, mule deer, bighorn sheep, yellow-bellied marmot, pika

Highway 180 (Kings Canyon Scenic Byway) leads through Giant Sequoia National Monument, along the South Fork of the Kings River, to the Cedar Grove Visitor Center in Kings Canyon. This spectacular glacier-sculpted canyon is traversed by a 6-mile dead-end road providing access to several attractions. Roaring River Falls, reached by a short, easy trail, is an impressive cascade rushing through a rocky granite canyon to a small pool. The 1.5-mile Zumwalt Meadow Trail makes

The South Fork of the Kings River flows placidly through Zumwalt Meadow in Kings Canyon National Park. Tall granite cliffs rise above the stream, which winds through a valley shaped by glacial action. Most of the national park is designated wilderness, accessible only to hikers and horseback riders.

for a relaxing and wonderfully scenic walk, with tall cliffs overhead and the Kings River flowing gently through broad meadows.

The road ends at appropriately named Road's End, under massive granite walls and peaks such as Grand Sentinel and North Dome. Many trails begin here and continue deep into the park's backcountry. A popular day hike leads 4 miles to Mist Falls, one of the largest waterfalls in the park. Along the way, the trail passes beautiful small cascades along the South Fork of the Kings River.

Returning back westward through Kings Canyon, drivers can take the unpaved, 3-mile River Road, which parallels the South Fork and provides a taste of what travel was like in the early days of the national park.

The imposing face of El Capitan, the world's largest granite monolith, dominates the north side of Yosemite Valley, with the distinctive shape of Half Dome rising in the distance. Seven miles long and one mile wide, Yosemite Valley is the starting point for the national park's most popular activities.

YOSEMITE NATIONAL PARK

BEAUTY IS INDEED A SUBJECTIVE IDEA, YET it is impossible to imagine anyone failing to agree that Yosemite Valley ranks among the most sublimely beautiful places on Earth. With its awe-inspiring waterfalls and imposing granite peaks, it offers an incomparable collection of vistas, each seemingly more breathtaking than the last. An early park official recalled the way many first-time visitors stood silent and tearful, "overwhelmed in the sudden presence of the unspeakable, stupendous grandeur."

And yet Yosemite Valley is only a small part of Yosemite National Park, which also encompasses alpine lakes and meadows, beautiful rivers, and groves of giant sequoia trees, the Earth's largest living things. In addition to its natural wonders, Yosemite has long been a landmark in conservation. Set aside as public land in 1864, Yosemite was the world's first wilderness preserve. Legendary conservationist John Muir fought for the creation of a national park here in 1890, and escorted President Theodore Roosevelt on a camping trip in 1903 that led to the park's expansion. Later in the 20th century, famed photographer Ansel Adams captured images of Yosemite that endure as icons of nature photography.

The prime destination for the national park's 3.5 million annual visitors is Yosemite Valley, 7 miles long and 1 mile wide. This valley contains not only the park's most famous natural features but developments such as visitor centers, camping, lodging, and stores. El Portal Road enters the valley from the west before dividing into one-way routes, one on each side of the Merced River. Once a lake, the valley has over time filled with sediment, leaving the broad, flat floor seen today.

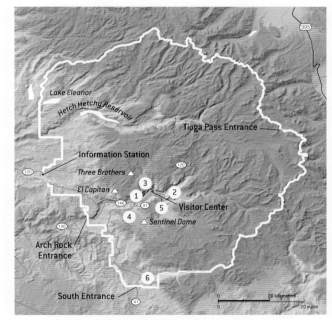

YOSEMITE CALIFORNIA

AREA
759,539 acres (3,074 sq km)
ESTABLISHED
October 1890
VISITOR INFORMATION
(209) 372 0200;
www.nps.gov/yose

KEY ATTRACTIONS ① Yosemite Valley ② Half Dome ③ Yosemite Falls ④ Bridalveil Falls ⑤ Glacier Point ⑥ Mariposa Grove
NOTABLE WILDLIFE Black bear, mule deer, bighorn sheep, mountain lion, spotted owl

Rising to the north is the massive blocky face of El Capitan, the world's largest granite monolith. Yosemite's geological history, including the predominance of granite and the shaping force of ice-age glaciation, is responsible for spectacular landforms such as its distinctively shaped peaks.

The waterfall first seen by most park visitors is 620-foot Bridalveil Falls, on the opposite side of the valley from El Capitan. Plunging over a sheer cliff and bursting into clouds of mist, Bridalveil can be reached by a short trail from a signed parking area. Nearby rise the aptly named Cathedral Rocks, showing an almost architectural verticality of form.

Nearer to Yosemite Village, the valley is dominated by breathtaking Yosemite Falls, dropping through a gap in a massive cliff on the north side. Composed of three separate falls—Upper Yosemite Fall (1,430 feet), Middle Cascades (675 feet), and Lower Yosemite Fall (320 feet)—this waterfall in its total height is among the tallest in the world. A 1-mile trail leads to a viewpoint of the Lower Fall, while a much more strenuous all-day hike leads to the Upper Fall.

The view to the east takes in the single most renowned image of Yosemite: the sheer-sided granite peak called Half Dome. The subject of some of Ansel Adams's most famous photographic studies, Half Dome looks as if it had been sliced by glacial action, though its sheer face is actually the result of fracturing along vertical joints. Erosion is a continuing process in Yosemite, with regular major rockfalls destroying swaths of forest and occasionally damaging park structures.

The climb to the top of Half Dome is a popular trek despite the difficulty of the ascent, with hikers using cables to assist near the steep summit. Easier, but still strenuous, trails lead to two beautiful waterfalls along the Merced River: 317-foot Vernal Fall and 594-foot Nevada Fall.

The Wawona Road leaves Yosemite Valley to reach the southern part of the park, climbing to quickly arrive at a tunnel. Just before that site is the Tunnel Overlook, a highly popular viewpoint for what has become the classic photograph of Yosemite Valley, with El Capitan on the left, Bridalveil Falls on the right, and Half Dome in the distance. A steep trail leads 1.3 miles to Inspiration Point, a higher and less crowded viewpoint looking east into the valley.

Continuing south, Wawona Road intersects with Glacier Point Road, a dead-end side route leading to the far-reaching vista at Glacier Point, 3,200 feet above Yosemite Valley. The panorama here, arguably one of the finest in North America, includes an unobstructed view of all of Yosemite Falls, as well as the meandering Merced River, Vernal and Nevada Falls, Half Dome, and the distant Tenaya Valley.

The most notable feature of Yosemite's Wawona area is Mariposa Grove, the park's most expansive forest of giant sequoias. Surviving 3,000 years or more, these magnificent trees are the largest living things on the planet in terms of volume (coast redwoods are taller). The 500 giant sequoias of Mariposa Grove include the Grizzly Giant, 210 feet tall with a circumference of almost 100 feet; the California Tunnel Tree, with a walk-through "tunnel" cut in its base; and the Wawona Tunnel Tree, which had a tunnel large enough for vehicles to drive through, but which fell in a snowstorm in 1969.

At 317 feet high, Vernal Fall ranks with the most spectacular waterfalls in Yosemite. A hike of around 1.5 miles ascends to the top of the cascade, finishing with a granite stairway of more than 600 steps. A less strenuous hike of 0.75 miles leads to a fine view of the fall from a footbridge over the Merced River.

Hikers reach the top of 8,836-foot Half Dome on an all-day hike of 14 or 16 miles round trip, depending on the route. Steel cables assist hikers on the last section, a 400-foot ascent along a very steep granite rock face. Climbing Half Dome is not recommended if the forecast includes a chance of rain or lightning.

In one of Yosemite National Park's classic scenes, Half Dome is reflected in the water of Mirror Lake as sunset reddens the granite rock face. Although some visitors imagine Half Dome was "sliced" by a glacier moving along the Tenaya Valley, its sheer face is the result of fracturing along joints in the rock.

Two other groves of giant sequoias, both smaller than Mariposa Grove but less visited, can be accessed at the western end of Tioga Road in the Crane Flat area, northwest of Yosemite Valley. Tuolumne and Merced Groves are both reached by moderately strenuous hikes and boast impressively sized trees.

The main attraction for most visitors in the northern part of the park is Tioga Road, which crosses the park from west to east and rises to a height of 9,945 feet at Tioga Pass. Panoramas along this route are spectacular, looking down into glacier-cut valleys and across mountain peaks rising above the treeline. The view from 8,400-foot Olmsted Point may be the highlight of Tioga Road, overlooking Tenaya Lake, the peak called Cloud's Rest, and Half Dome. Easy trails follow the shoreline of Tenaya Lake, one of the park's prettiest lakes, accessible along Tioga Road.

Almost 95 percent of the park's 1,187 square miles has been designated as wilderness, crisscrossed by trails providing ample opportunity for backpackers to escape roads and other development. Yosemite is crossed north–south by the Pacific Crest National Scenic Trail, which runs more than 2,600 miles from Mexico to Canada.

LASSEN VOLCANIC NATIONAL PARK

A LIVING GEOLOGY TEXTBOOK, LASSEN Volcanic National Park offers visitors the chance to explore a volcanic landscape in action: Fumaroles emit sulphur-laden volcanic gas, mudholes burble, pools of water boil, and steam rises from the ground. At the center of the park stands 10,457-foot Lassen Peak, a volcano that erupted violently in May, 1915, devastating a vast surrounding area and raining ash on places 200 miles away. Still an active volcano, though temporarily dormant, Lassen looms over the rugged, wooded park, a reminder that it occupies a place in the famed Pacific "Ring of Fire" region of volcanic and earthquake activity.

Lassen lies at the southern end of the Cascade Range, volcanic mountains that stretch from northern California northward into British Columbia. A place of lush coniferous forests, beautiful lakes, striking peaks, and heavy winter snows, the Cascades include around 20 major volcanoes. The most recent significant Cascades eruption was the massive explosion of Mount St. Helens in Washington in 1980.

Visitors entering the national park from the south should stop at the Kohm Yah-mah-nee Visitor Center, a highly energy-efficient building opened in 2008, before continuing to sites such as Sulphur Works and Bumpass Hell. The latter, the park's largest concentration of hydrothermal features, is traversed by a 1.5-mile trail through a stark landscape of scattered trees among barren earth stained yellowish by sulphur emissions.

After passing Lake Helen, one of the park's prettiest lakes, the main road reaches a turnoff to the trailhead for the strenuous 5-mile round-trip hike up Lassen Peak. The view from the top takes in the well-named Devastated Area to the immediate northeast, where the tremendous 1915 explosion flattened everything in its path. Lassen Peak's panorama also encompasses dozens of lower summits, as well as mountain lakes and forest. More than 30 different volcanoes have erupted within what is now the park boundary in the past 300,000

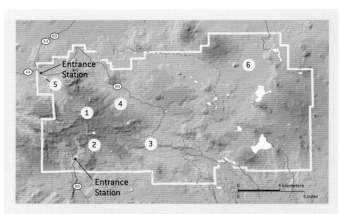

LASSEN VOLCANIC NORTHERN CALIFORNIA

AREA
106,368 acres (430 sq km)

ESTABLISHED
August 1916

VISITOR INFORMATION
(530) 595 4480;
www.nps.gov/lavo

KEY ATTRACTIONS ① Lassen Peak
② Bumpass Hell ③ Kings Creek
Falls ④ Devastated Area ⑤
Manzanita Lake ⑥ Cinder Cone

NOTABLE WILDLIFE Black bear,
mule deer, yellow-bellied marmot,
pika, white-headed woodpecker

A boardwalk along a 3-mile round-trip trail allows hikers to get close looks at the landscape of Bumpass Hell, the largest concentration of hydrothermal features in the park. Steam from Big Boiler, the largest fumarole in the park, has been measured at a temperature as high as 322°F (161°C).

years. All four types of volcanoes are found in Lassen Volcanic National Park: shield (large and with shallow-sloping sides), lava dome (a circular mound shape resulting from slow lava flow), cinder cone (a conical hill of volcanic fragments around a vent), and composite (tall and conical with many layers of hardened lava, tephra, and volcanic ash).

The 29-mile park road, the highest vehicle route in the Cascade Range, reaches a high point of 8,512 feet near Lassen Peak. (Heavy snow means the road can be closed as much as eight months of the year.) Farther along the route, a 3-mile trail leads to splendid Kings Creek Falls, a broad waterfall dropping over a series of rock ledges, well worth the moderately strenuous trek to see it. The road then reaches the short, easy nature trail at the Devastated Area, which features interpretive signs on the violent events of 1915.

One of the park's most striking landscapes is that of Chaos Crags, a group of tall lava domes, and Chaos Jumble, a large field of rocks formed when a lava dome collapsed several hundred years ago. The event blocked a creek, forming Manzanita Lake at the park's northwestern corner. This beautiful lake is surrounded by forests of willow, mountain alder, Jeffrey pine, white fir, and lodgepole pine. The loop trail around the lake is popular with birdwatchers.

A 2-mile hike in the park's northeastern corner leads to the symmetrical volcanic feature called Cinder Cone, a 700-foot-high mound of black scoria (bits of lava thrown into the air during an eruption) that formed about 350 years ago. Nearby are the Painted Dunes, lava flows showing colorful orange hues from oxidation of minerals. The trek to the top of Cinder Cone is steep, but the summit offers yet another of Lassen Volcanic National Park's many superb and otherworldly vistas.

Soaring to heights over 360 feet, coast redwoods rank as the tallest trees on Earth. The species' requirements of adequate year-round moisture, moderate temperatures, and other exacting environmental factors mean they grow only in a limited range along the Pacific Coast of North America.

REDWOOD NATIONAL AND STATE PARKS

THE TALLEST TREES ON EARTH, COAST redwoods grow only in a narrow strip of land along the Pacific Ocean in northwestern California and southwestern Oregon. Exceptional specimens of this species can top 360 feet in height, with the tallest known redwood reaching 379 feet. Unfortunately, the massive size and excellent timber of redwoods made them targets for 19th-century loggers, and as early as the first decades of the 20th century, conservationists were expressing concern about their disappearance.

California created three state parks in the 1920s to protect redwood forests, and Redwood National Park was established in 1968. In 1994, all four parks were combined for administrative purposes, forming a unique federal-state partnership to better manage their lands. Today, only about 4 percent of the original coast redwood ecosystem remains in its natural condition. Redwood National and State Parks encompasses 45 percent of the existing old-growth redwood forest, as well as 37 miles of beautiful Pacific Ocean shoreline.

The woodlands here truly deserve the adjective "awe-inspiring." Redwood trunks soar to dizzying heights beside trails and roads, their thick bark helping them resist disease, fire, and insects. Some redwoods can live 2,000 years or more. Yet this ecosystem is notable for much more than this single species. Here, too, grow Douglas-fir, Sitka spruce, tanoak, madrone, and Jeffrey pine, as well as masses of spectacular rhododendrons, blooming from mid-May into June. Designated both a World Heritage Site and an International Biosphere Reserve, Redwood National and State Parks provides a home to an array of threatened and endangered plants and animals.

Many visitors enter the park from the south along scenic U.S. Highway 101, from which Bald Hills Road leads east 2 miles to Lady Bird Johnson Grove, named for the former First Lady and

Magnificent Roosevelt elk are seen most often in the park's prairie areas, where they graze on the abundant grasses and herbs. Elk are most active at dawn and dusk. Males can be 10 feet long and weigh 1,000 pounds; they engage in fights during the fall breeding season for access to females.

active conservationist. An easy trail loops through a glorious forest of old-growth redwoods, Douglas-firs, and tanoaks. In spring, rhododendrons and azaleas display their pinkish flowers, and maples show brilliant foliage in fall.

Farther north, Davison Road leads west to beautiful Gold Bluffs Beach and the short loop trail through Fern Canyon, where dense fern growth covering 30-foot-high rock walls creates a scene of breathtaking lushness. Impressively large Roosevelt elk might be seen along Davison Road or just north in Prairie Creek Redwoods State Park.

Newton B. Drury Scenic Parkway, a 10-mile route paralleling Highway 101, passes among magnificent redwoods and provides access to some of the parks' finest groves of old-growth trees. A short, easy trail leads to Big Tree Wayside, and nearby are trailheads for fabulous hikes such as the 1.4-mile Cathedral Trees Trail and the 4-mile Prairie Creek Trail.

Farther north, Coastal Drive is an 8-mile unpaved side road with some of the finest views along the California coast. Apart

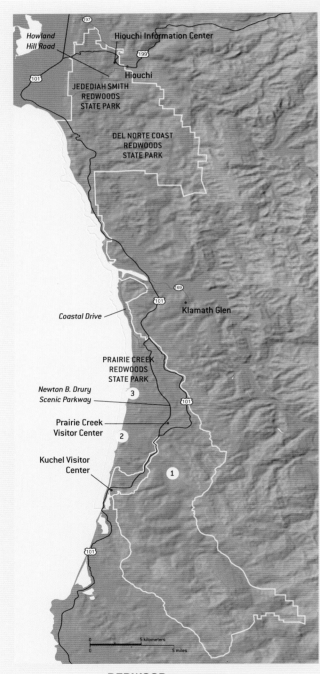

REDWOOD CALIFORNIA

AREA
131,983 acres (534 sq km)
ESTABLISHED
October 1968
VISITOR INFORMATION
(707) 464 6101;
www.nps.gov/redw

KEY ATTRACTIONS ① Lady Bird Johnson Grove ② Gold Bluffs Beach ③ Fern Canyon
NOTABLE WILDLIFE Roosevelt elk, black bear, mountain lion, California sea lion, gray whale, harbor seal, spotted owl, marbled murrelet

Found along the North American Pacific Coast from Mexico to Alaska's Aleutian Islands, the black oystercatcher is one of the most striking bird residents of the park's rocky shores. Pairs may occupy the same area of coast for years, feeding mostly on molluscs such as mussels and limpets.

from the landscape of beach, sea, and wave-battered rocks, this route offers the chance to see wildlife including sea lions and brown pelicans. Sea stacks (small rocky islands) give seabirds protection from predators, and thousands of gulls, guillemots, cormorants, and other colonial-nesting birds breed along this stretch of coast. From viewpoints here, and from the Klamath River Overlook to the north, migrating gray whales can be spotted in spring and fall.

Highway 101 continues north to Del Norte Coast Redwoods State Park and Enderts Beach Road. Crescent Beach Overlook offers another fine point from which to scan for whales and seabirds, while the Coastal Trail leads to Enderts Beach, an excellent place to enjoy the colorful world of tidepools. Park rangers give regular programs here revealing creatures such as seastars, limpets, anemones, and crabs.

The Coastal Trail consists of several sections that wind almost the length of the combined parks along the Pacific Ocean shore, for a total distance of 70 miles. Alternating between ridges above the water and stretches of beach hiking, this route provides some of the parks' most enjoyable walks, although visitors should be aware of tide times and of the dangers of powerful waves that crash along the beach.

Some of the region's most majestic stands of coast redwoods can be enjoyed in Jedediah Smith Redwoods State Park, the

northernmost unit of the combined National and State Parks. Howland Hill Road is a narrow, winding, unpaved 6-mile route through mature redwoods, with many pullouts for viewing tall trees. The Stout Memorial Grove Trail and the Boy Scout Tree Trail, both beginning along Howland Hill Road, wind among old-growth redwoods, some over 300 feet high. The River Trail follows the Jedediah Smith River, the last major undammed river in California, through old-growth redwood forest. Steelhead trout and chinook salmon abound in the beautiful stream.

Winters can be very rainy along this section of the Pacific Coast, and summer brings times of dense fog. While these conditions may temporarily impede activities in the parks, they are vital for the existence of the coast redwood forest. Redwoods grow only in areas close enough to the ocean that fog forms on summer nights, condensing on the trees and providing them with moisture in what is otherwise a dry season. The abundant precipitation of rain, fog, and occasional snow in combination (more than 100 inches annually) is one of the factors allowing redwoods to grow taller than any other tree species.

Scientists still do not have all the answers that could explain the incredible size of coast redwoods. They have survived in their current range on the Pacific Coast for 20 million years, though, and their ancestors were around during the age of the dinosaurs, more than 150 million years ago.

Crater Lake receives up to 44 feet of snow each winter. The park's Rim Drive, which circles the lake, closes for several months between fall and summer. The park remains open year-round, though—its scenery, already spectacular, takes on a different aspect when snow covers the landscape.

CRATER LAKE NATIONAL PARK

FOR SHEER DRAMATIC IMPACT OF A SINGLE panorama, few national parks can top the view of Crater Lake from its rim: the encircling cliffs, the cone of Wizard Island rising near the western shore, and, most especially, the overwhelmingly intense blue of its water, a color so rich that it truly can be called incomparable.

The beauty of the modern scene contrasts sharply with the violence of its geological origin. On this spot stood a volcano that scientists call Mount Mazama, built from hundreds of thousands of years of eruptions and possibly rising as high as 12,000 feet. Like Mount Rainier, Mount St. Helens, and Lassen Peak, it was (and is) part of the volcanically active Cascade Range. Around 7,700 years ago, Mazama exploded in an eruption so powerful that the top of the volcano collapsed into the empty magma chamber, forming a huge, deep caldera. In the millennia since that event, rain and snowmelt have filled the caldera with water of great purity, creating a lake 1,943 feet deep—the deepest lake in the United States and the seventh deepest in the world. The lake's depth was measured first in 1886 by the simple means of attaching a weight to a spool of piano wire and lowering it into the lake at 168 different places. Those early surveyors recorded a depth of 1,996 feet—an error of less than 3 percent from the figure revealed by modern equipment.

It is the combination of Crater Lake's pristine water quality and depth that give its blue such a vivid hue. Lake water absorbs every color except blue, reflecting that shade back to the viewer's eyes with startling brilliance. (Three gold prospectors who chanced upon the lake in 1853

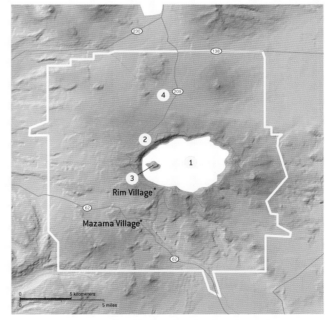

CRATER LAKE OREGON

AREA
183,224 acres (741 sq km)

ESTABLISHED
May 1902

VISITOR INFORMATION
(541) 594 3000;
www.nps.gov/crla

KEY ATTRACTIONS ① Crater Lake
② Rim Drive ③ Wizard Island
④ Pumice Desert

NOTABLE WILDLIFE Roosevelt elk, black bear, mule deer, black-tailed deer, pronghorn, American marten, porcupine

proposed naming it Deep Blue Lake.) Tests have shown Crater Lake's water to rank among the purest and most translucent on Earth.

The park's southern entrance road winds up the flank of ancient Mount Mazama, arriving at the Rim Village area for the first opportunity to admire Crater Lake. The Sinnott Memorial Overlook, perched on the rim of the caldera, provides a classic view of the lake, with Wizard Island prominent in the scene. Wizard is actually a cinder cone built by a volcanic vent in Mount Mazama's caldera after it collapsed, and was named for its resemblance to the pointed hat often depicted on old-time magicians. Wizard Island is one of many park features named by William Gladstone Steel, who spent decades of his life and much of his fortune in the effort to establish Crater Lake National Park and provide visitor services in its early years.

Visitors who would like an even higher viewpoint of the lake and the surrounding region (including the Klamath Basin and Mount Shasta) can hike the strenuous 1.7-mile trail to the top of Garfield Peak, gaining just over 1,000 feet in elevation while following the caldera rim.

Crater Lake National Park's Rim Drive circles the lake on its 33-mile route, with many overlooks offering views from different perspectives. Crater Lake receives an average of more than 44 feet of snow each winter, and Rim Drive may not open for the summer until late June or July. Nonetheless, the park stays open year-round (though many facilities are closed), and for visitors prepared to deal with the severe conditions, the snow-covered landscape creates scenes of breathtaking beauty.

Taking Rim Drive clockwise from Rim Village, drivers reach Discovery Point in just a mile or so. Here, in 1853, prospector John Wesley Hillman was among the first European-Americans to see Crater Lake. Another 2 miles along the drive brings the trailhead for the very steep hike up The Watchman, gaining 650 feet in 0.7 miles. Dikes of magma here flowed from vents of Mount Mazama.

Cleetwood Cove, on the north side of Crater Lake, is the only spot where visitors are allowed to hike down to the shoreline. A strenuous 1.1-mile trail descends to the water, where anglers fish for rainbow trout and kokanee salmon (both species present as a result of early stocking programs). Most of those who hike this trail, though, do so to take a guided boat tour of Crater Lake, offered in summer only from a dock at Cleetwood Cove. Park rangers provide commentary on geology, nature, and history as the boat circles the lake. Another tour option

The American marten, a member of the weasel family, inhabits forests from Alaska to Newfoundland and south in the mountains of the American West. Quick, agile, and able to climb trees well, it feeds on mammals such as squirrels and snowshoe hares, as well as birds and their eggs.

involves disembarking at Wizard Island for a half-day or full day of exploring this volcanic cone. The 0.9-mile Wizard Summit Trail climbs the cone for a look at the 90-foot-deep crater at its top.

Rim Drive continues past more picnic areas and overlooks, including Phantom Ship Overlook, which provides a good view of Crater Lake's smaller island, a jagged speck of land that does indeed resemble a sailing craft. Several of the overlooks offer superb views of the tall cliffs that ring the lake, some rising as high as 2,000 feet over the water. As a point of geographic reference, the tallest cliffs around Crater Lake are approximately as high as the lake is deep.

A 6-mile side road off Rim Drive leads down glacier-carved Kerr Valley for a view of the Pinnacles, strikingly pointed columnar formations of hardened volcanic material. One of the park's most popular short trails can be found along Rim Drive just before it returns to Steel Information Center. The Castle Crest Wildflower Garden Trail is an easy 0.4-mile loop passing along a brook and through a meadow that blazes with multicolored flowers in the brief summer growing season.

Another world awaits travelers who take the road from Crater Lake's North Junction to the park's northern entrance. This route crosses the Pumice Desert, where volcanic material from the eruption of Mount Mazama covers the ground to a depth of 50 feet. Precipitation drains through the soil so quickly that few plants can grow here, giving the landscape the stark appearance of a desert. Volcanic cones dot this barren-looking landscape, their flanks covered in pine forest. Timber Crater, 7,424 feet high, is the tallest cinder cone in Crater Lake National Park.

The national park was established before large-scale commercial logging affected the Crater Lake area, which means that coniferous forests here are mostly old growth, from ponderosa pine at low elevation up through lodgepole pine and mountain hemlock to whitebark pine on the highest mountain slopes. One of the park's most notable mammal residents is the Roosevelt elk, with some males weighing 1,000 pounds or more.

Crater Lake National Park is known as an excellent birdwatching site, with a long list of species typical of the northwestern United States mountains, such as rufous hummingbirds, black-backed woodpeckers, olive-sided flycatchers, gray and Steller's jays, Clark's nutcrackers, varied thrushes, and mountain chickadees. Lucky birders might even find a rarity such as a spotted owl or a three-toed woodpecker.

Wizard Island comprises the top of a cinder cone that formed after the creation of the main volcanic caldera 7,700 years ago. Visitors can take a concessioner-operated boat to the island and hike a 0.9-mile trail that ascends 750 feet to its summit, marked by a 90-foot-deep crater.

A member of the crow family, the Clark's nutcracker was named for William Clark of the famed Lewis and Clark Expedition, who first observed it in 1805. The Clark's nutcracker feeds mostly on pine seeds, which it stores in caches. Its long, strong bill enables it to open pine cones to reach seeds.

MOUNT RAINIER NATIONAL PARK

FOR RESIDENTS OF WESTERN WASHINGTON, a daily ritual is the glance toward Mount Rainier to see if the snow-capped summit of "The Mountain" is visible through the clouds. Like a white beacon above the rest of the Cascade Range, Rainier attracts travelers eager to explore its dense forests, wildflower-filled meadows, rushing waterfalls, and alpine landscapes. Thousands annually challenge its icy slopes in attempts to reach its 14,410-foot peak, while others are content simply to look upward and admire its rugged face.

Part of the highly volcanic Pacific "Ring of Fire" zone of frequent earthquakes and eruptions, Mount Rainier is an active volcano. It began growing about 500,000 years ago, as lava flows built one atop another until they formed a huge cone of the type called a composite. At one time, Rainier may have risen 2,000 feet higher than its present stature, only to lose parts of its summit to glacial action, eruptions, and collapses of rock walls. Rainier's most recent eruptions occurred in the first half of the 19th century, though steam and gas still escape from vents. In the words of park geologists, Rainier is "sleeping, not dead."

Today, Mount Rainier National Park is home to the largest group of glaciers found on a single mountain in the lower 48 states, with 25 major glaciers and many snow- and icefields. (This despite the fact that Rainier's glaciers shrank by 25 percent between 1913 and 1994.) The largest, Emmons Glacier, covers an area of 4.3 square miles. It is common for the park to receive 50 feet of snow each winter; in 1998–99 the total was

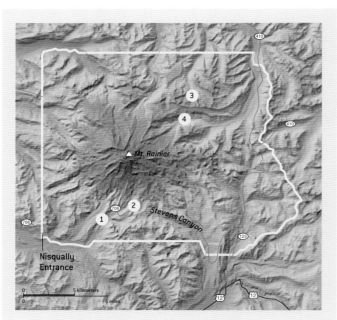

MOUNT RAINIER WASHINGTON

AREA
235,670 acres (954 sq km)

ESTABLISHED
March 1899

VISITOR INFORMATION
(360) 569 2211;
www.nps.gov/mora

KEY ATTRACTIONS ① Longmire National Historic Landmark District ② Paradise ③ Sunrise ④ Emmons Glacier

NOTABLE WILDLIFE Mountain goat, elk, black-tailed deer, black bear, hoary marmot

Lupines and asters highlight a wildflower meadow below the rugged slopes of Mount Rainier, home to more glaciers than any other mountain in the lower 48 states. Some winters receiving more than 80 feet of snow, the park has only a brief summer growing season for its diverse plant life.

At the breathtaking Grove of the Patriarchs, a boardwalk makes up part of the 1.3-mile nature trail along the Ohanapecosh River. The path passes through old-growth forest of Douglas-fir, western hemlock, and western red-cedar. Ohanapecosh is a Cowlitz Native American word thought to mean "standing on the edge."

Hoary marmots are large, chunky squirrels often seen in open areas of Mount Rainier National Park. On summer days, marmots spend time sunning themselves, leaving the burrows where they hibernate for much of the year.

more than 86 feet. Some park roads may not open until July, when this massive snowfall finally melts enough to allow vehicles. The road from the Nisqually entrance to the popular Paradise area is kept open all year.

Two areas along the Nisqually Road demonstrate the way Mount Rainier reshapes itself. The Westside Road along Tahoma Creek and a trail at Kautz Creek both reveal evidence of flash floods, rockfalls, and debris flows that remain regular occurrences in the park. The short, easy Twin Firs Trail passes through an old-growth forest of Douglas-fir, western red-cedar, and hemlock. Ahead lies the Longmire area, site of an early resort and rustic-style park administrative buildings, now a federally designated National Historic District.

Nisqually Road also passes trailheads for viewing some of the park's beautiful waterfalls, including Carter Falls, Christine Falls, Comet Falls, and Narada Falls. Some are easy walks, while seeing Comet Falls requires a round trip of 3.6 miles.

Paradise ranks as by far the park's most popular destination, set on the southern flank of Mount Rainier at an elevation of 5,400 feet. The main visitor center is here, and hiking trails lead from Paradise to gorgeous mountain lakes, waterfalls, and vistas of glaciers and expansive valleys—and, of course, to even closer views of Mount Rainier, its barren rock ridges bordered by glaciers and snowfields. The Skyline Loop is a 5.5-mile hike

that ascends to 6,400-foot Panorama Point, well named for the fabulous views of Rainier, Nisqually Glacier, and distant peaks including the summits of the Tatoosh Range to the south.

Stevens Canyon Road leaves the Paradise area eastward, passing by Reflection Lake, named for the striking mirror-like view of Rainier reflected in its water on calm days. Just beyond is the trailhead for a rewarding hike to Bench and Snow Lakes. This 2.5-mile round-trip walk crosses low ridges to reach the lakes, with abundant summer wildflowers along the way. The meadows around the lakes are likely places to spot black bears in late summer when berries ripen.

Stevens Canyon is a classic U-shaped valley created by a moving glacier, which cut back into canyon walls to form "hanging valleys" like that of Unicorn Creek, where Martha Falls cascades over a rock ledge to the canyon floor. Running alongside Stevens Creek is one segment of the Wonderland Trail, the national park's ultimate long-distance trek. Circling Mount Rainier on a route 93 miles long, the Wonderland Trail requires frequent climbs of 3,000 feet or more, and features more than 20 campsites scattered along the circuit.

The road continues to Box Canyon, with a dramatic vista of the Cowlitz River rushing through a narrow gorge eroded 180 feet down into bedrock. After curving south around Backbone Ridge, Stevens Canyon Road reaches the Grove of the

Patriarchs, where an easy 1.3-mile trail loops through an awe-inspiring forest of Douglas-firs and red-cedars, some of them 1,000 years old. At nearby Silver Falls, among the park's best waterfalls, the Ohanapecosh River surges between rock walls at a site a 0.3-mile walk from the road.

In the northeastern part of the park, a side road off Highway 410 leads along the White River and up Sunrise Ridge to the Sunrise Visitor Center. At 6,400 feet, this is the highest point in the park reached by road. This area, open only in summer, is a popular gateway to exploring Mount Rainier National Park's high country and glaciers, with a network of trails offering many opportunities for backcountry travel. It is only a half-mile walk to Emmons Vista, a viewpoint overlooking the park's largest glacier, with Columbia Crest, Rainier's summit, looming beyond. The Sourdough Ridge Trail is a 1-mile loop through meadows bordered by conifers stunted by growing conditions at the treeline, with views of other Cascade Range peaks such as Mount Baker and Mount Adams. On these and other Sunrise trails, hikers should watch for mountain goats, which scramble along slopes seemingly too steep to provide places to step.

More than 80 square miles of Mount Rainier National Park lies in the alpine zone, at elevations too high for trees to grow. This habitat is home to the white-tailed ptarmigan, a grouse-like bird that changes its plumage from pure white in winter to a mottled brown in summer, as seen here.

Mist blankets the seascape at Shi Shi Beach, on the northern stretch of Olympic's 73 miles of Pacific Ocean coastline. Although best known for its mountains and rain forests, the park also protects gorgeous stretches of pristine beaches, as well as offshore rocks providing nesting areas for seabirds.

OLYMPIC
NATIONAL PARK

ONE OF THE MOST BEAUTIFUL AND distinctive landscapes in the United States covers the western slopes of Washington's Olympic Mountains. Nourished by rainfall that can total more than 160 inches a year, the temperate rain forest that grows here boasts massive trees towering over an understory in which nearly every square inch is filled with ferns, mosses, and other plants, creating enchanting scenes of lush greenery.

Yet Olympic National Park encompasses far more than the verdant world of the temperate rain forest. At its center rise the rugged, snow-capped Olympic Mountains. Highest of them is 7,980-foot Mount Olympus, in part blanketed by the third-largest collection of glaciers in the lower 48 states. No roads reach the heart of these mountains, which comprise part of the park's 1,350 square miles of federally designated wilderness (95 percent of the park land area).

A separate unit of Olympic National Park protects 73 miles of Pacific Ocean coastline, a place of sandy beaches, rocky headlands, and tidepools full of colorful sea creatures. Seals, sea otters, and many species of seabirds make their homes along this coast, much of which is also an official wilderness area.

The park's diverse ecological resources, as well as a significant number of rare plants and animals found nowhere else on Earth, have led to its designation as both a World Heritage Site and an International Biosphere Reserve.

After stopping at park headquarters in the town of Port Angeles, most visitors make the 45-minute drive up to the Hurricane Ridge Visitor Center, at an elevation of 5,242 feet. Named for winds that can blow 75 miles per hour at times, this popular site is reached by a winding road that passes from lowland forest to treeline, where subalpine fir survives harsh

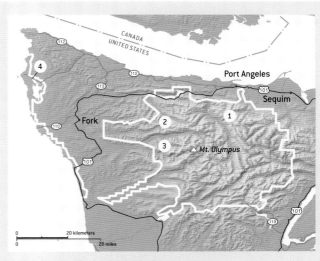

OLYMPIC WASHINGTON

AREA
922,651 acres (3,734 sq km)
ESTABLISHED
June 1938
VISITOR INFORMATION
(360) 565 3130;
www.nps.gov/olym

KEY ATTRACTIONS ① Hurricane Ridge ② Sol Duc Valley ③ Hoh Valley ④ Ozette
NOTABLE WILDLIFE Roosevelt elk, black-tailed deer, black bear, Olympic marmot, mountain lion

conditions that include more than 30 feet of winter snow. Easy trails provide access to overlooks with excellent views of the Strait of Juan de Fuca to the north and the Bailey Range of the Olympic Mountains to the south. A 1.6-mile trail leads to Hurricane Hill, for an even more all-encompassing panorama. When conditions are right, the Pacific Ocean can be seen 33 miles to the west.

Hikers admiring the meadows of wildflowers around Hurricane Ridge might spot an Olympic marmot, a rodent found only in the Olympic Mountains. The marmot is one of several species of fauna and flora that evolved here, separated from related species by eons of glaciation, changing sea levels, and geographic isolation. Other endemic species include a salamander, a fish, a grasshopper, seveal beetles, and the Olympic snow mole, a subspecies of the Townsend's mole that lives in alpine habitat above the treeline.

Two unpaved routes, the Obstruction Point and Deer Park Roads, allow drivers to explore more extensive areas in the park's alpine zone. Obstruction Point Road travels east from the Hurricane Ridge area, while Deer Park Road is reached off U.S. Highway 101 east of Port Angeles.

Farther west, off U.S. Highway 101, side roads lead into the valleys of the Elwha and Sol Duc Rivers. The Elwha was altered in the 20th century by two dams that are now being removed to allow the historic salmon fishery to recover; all five species of Pacific salmon are expected to return to the river. The Elwha River restoration project is the second-largest habitat restoration effort in the history of the National Park Service. Along the entrance road through the Elwha Valley is the short, easy stroll to 60-foot-high Madison Falls. Other trails include a 2.5-mile hike through a beautiful forest of Douglas-fir and western red-cedar to Olympic Hot Springs, a popular natural "spa."

Sol Duc is a Quileute Native American name meaning "sparkling water," and the Sol Duc River does indeed sparkle as it rushes along its rocky course where coho salmon and other species swim upstream to breed. A 0.8-mile trail leads to an observation platform beside beautiful Sol Duc Falls, and an easy 0.6-mile loop called the Ancient Groves Trail winds through impressive lowland old-growth forest.

The western side of Olympic Mountains ranks among the rainiest places in the United States, and it is this abundant moisture, along with moderate temperatures, that sustains the magnificent temperate rain forests of the national park's Bogachiel, Hoh, Queets, and Quinault Valleys. Sitka spruce and western hemlock dominate the forests, growing with Douglas-fir, western red-cedar, and maples. Epiphytes (plants that grow on other plants) drape every limb and cover the trunks of fallen trees, to such a degree that these forests actually have three times the total biomass of a tropical rain forest such as that in Amazonia.

Roads and trails lead into all four valleys, but the best place to get acquainted with the park's temperate rain forest is the Hoh Rain Forest Visitor Center, located along the river that begins high on the slopes of Mount Olympus. Short interpretive trails loop through this primeval forest, and adventurous hikers can tackle the 18-mile Hoh River Trail, which ascends to Blue Glacier, on the north side of Olympus.

Receiving around 160 inches of precipitation annually, the western slopes of the national park are among the rainiest places in the United States outside Hawaii. In the Hoh River Valley, abundant moisture encourages the growth of ferns and mosses that cover nearly every square inch of tree trunks and branches.

Giant green anemones and an ochre sea star are among the inhabitants of a tidepool along the Olympic National Park shore. Rangers lead regular beach walks at sites along the Pacific Coast, helping visitors understand the fascinating life that manages to survive in this wave-battered environment.

A female black-tailed deer watches warily from an Olympic hillside. Considered a subspecies of the mule deer, black-tails are common in the park, especially at the edges of woodland, where they can feed in adjacent meadows but retreat quickly into the forest in case of danger.

Several hundred Roosevelt elk live in the Hoh Valley, part of the total park population of as many as 5,000. Olympic National Park was created in part to protect these mammals (the largest subspecies of elk), as well as the forests of the Olympic Mountains. Grazing by elk helps keep the understory of the rain forest open, rather than crowded by vines and shrubs. Other large mammals found in the park include black bears, mountain lions, black-tailed deer, and coyotes.

Some of the most spectacular scenes in the park are found not in the rain forest or mountains but along the Pacific Ocean coast, where stretches of sandy beach are interrupted by picturesque points of rock reaching into the sea, with tall rock stacks rising just offshore. In places such as Rialto Beach and Ruby Beach, erosion has shaped rocks into spires and arches with almost sculptural qualities—though the puffins, auklets, cormorants, and murres that nest on them are most interested in the practical qualities of their isolation from predators.

From March to May, gray whales migrate along the Pacific Ocean coast, and may be seen from viewpoints along the shore. Sea otters were extirpated in the park area by overhunting, but after a reintroduction program several hundred now live offshore. Seals and sea lions also might be spotted from Olympic's shores.

One of the best places to enjoy the national park's Pacific coastline is the Ozette area, once the site of a Makah Native American village. A splendid 9-mile loop hike here passes through a prairie (once a pasture for livestock) to reach the beach, then returns through coastal forest.

At coastal locations such as Mora and Klaloch, park rangers lead regular walks to explore the spectacular animal residents of tidepools—less conspicuous, but just as fascinating, as the life of the forest. Visitors should check at visitor centers for times when tidepool programs are offered; when the tide is too high, rangers lead beach walks instead. Other ranger-led programs include forest and meadow walks and campfire talks.

NORTH CASCADES NATIONAL PARK

THE NORTH CASCADES RANGE IS A PLACE of rugged peaks, remote wilderness, high-country lakes, and rocky rivers rushing through beautiful wooded valleys. Barren mountain summits rise on the horizon like saw teeth, challenging hikers and rock climbers to explore their slopes. A hint of the nature of the terrain is found in names of landscape features: Mount Despair, Forbidden Peak, Mount Terror, Desolation Peak.

Yet despite the wild nature of much of the region, there are plenty of opportunities to enjoy its beauty on easy trails, boat trips, horseback rides, and guided walks led by park rangers. Many attractions are located along North Cascades Scenic Highway, an officially designated National Scenic Byway that runs through the heart of the park.

North Cascades National Park is administered as part of a larger area called North Cascades National Park Service Complex, which includes North and South Units of the national park and Ross Lake and Chelan Lake National Recreation Areas. The national park units have almost no development other than trails and backcountry campsites. Cascade River Road reaches the western boundary of the South Unit, providing access to the excellent hike to 5,384-foot Cascade Pass. Spectacular views from this area take in some of the park's more than 300 glaciers. (More than half the glaciers found in the lower 48 states lie within North Cascades National Park.)

Most visitors reach Lake Chelan National Recreation Area by taking a boat to the small resort community of Stehekin, which offers a visitor center, lodging, and trails to destinations including the deep gorge cut by Agnes Creek. The Pacific Crest National Scenic Trail, which runs 2,650 miles from Mexico to Canada, passes through the glacier-carved Stehekin Valley.

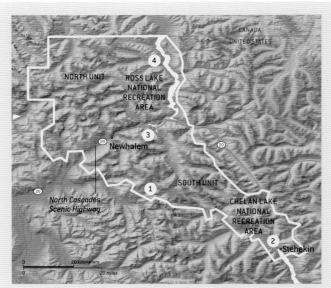

NORTH CASCADES WASHINGTON

AREA
504,781 acres (2,043 sq km)
ESTABLISHED
October 1968
VISITOR INFORMATION
(360) 854 7200;
www.nps.gov/noca

KEY ATTRACTIONS ① Cascades
Pass ② Lake Chelan ③ Diablo
Lake ④ Ross Lake
NOTABLE WILDLIFE Grizzly
bear, black bear, mountain
goat, gray wolf, mule deer, elk,
moose, lynx

The most popular destinations in the park complex lie within Ross Lake National Recreation Area, where the North Cascades National Park Visitor Center (near the community of Newhalem) is the best source of information about park activities. North Cascades Scenic Highway runs alongside the beautiful Skagit River, which in places just downstream from the park hosts significant numbers of wintering bald eagles.

Trails in the Newhalem area and upstream at Thunder Creek range from easy nature walks to long-distance backpacking trails leading to mountain passes with far-reaching views of the North Cascades. Hikers pass among massive western red-cedars and other trees of the old-growth forest at low elevations, ascending to alpine meadows that can be bright with wildflowers when snow melts in summer. A short trail leads to beautiful Ladder Creek Falls, a waterfall on the south side of the Skagit River near Newhalem.

Park rangers participate in commercial boat tours offered on Diablo Lake by Seattle City Light, the utility that built dams on the Skagit River to provide electrical power to the region. Offered in summer, these scenic tours depart from the Skagit Information Center in Newhalem, with rangers providing commentary on the geology and wildlife of the area as the boat cruises around Diablo Lake.

The Skagit River Valley is home to one of the largest concentrations of wintering bald eagles in the United States outside Alaska. Park rangers and volunteers conduct surveys of eagle numbers along the river, watching for long-term trends that provide evidence of the health of the population.

GLACIER BAY NATIONAL PARK AND PRESERVE

TRAVELERS WHO ENTER GLACIER BAY BY boat discover a landscape for which the word "breathtaking" seems hardly adequate. Snow-covered mountains rise all around; rugged, rocky islands dot the bay; and the glaciers for which the area was named stretch down valleys to the sea, creating formidable walls of ice and calving icebergs that float serenely on the blue water. Whales, bears, eagles, seals, and sea otters make up only part of the wildlife that might be seen in the water, on the shore, and in the sky.

Yet there is another side to Glacier Bay National Park and Preserve, apart from its obvious beauty. Scientists know the bay as a living laboratory of biological succession, thanks to its extraordinary recent history. As recently as 1750 (just a few ticks of Earth's geological clock), the entire bay was filled by a huge glacier that was up to 4,000 feet thick and had its origin 100 miles inland. By the time famed conservationist John Muir explored the bay in 1879, the glacier had retreated more than 30 miles, creating an expansive bay. Today, Glacier Bay extends 60 miles inland, with ice continuing to shrink in most areas.

The result: Both biologists and vacationers can experience a place where the Earth was scraped clean of all life, and an ecosystem is in the process of reconstituting itself. Moving inland in Glacier Bay is like traveling backwards in time. Near its mouth, where ice disappeared more than 200 years ago, a mature forest of Sitka spruce and hemlock grows. Farther up the bay are small willows, alders, and shrubs, and closer to the glaciers, where ice retreated just decades ago, only lichens have had time to re-establish themselves.

Many visitors see Glacier Bay as part of a cruise ship's journey along the coast of Alaska's Panhandle, with the park ranking as the highlight of a trip filled with spectacular scenery.

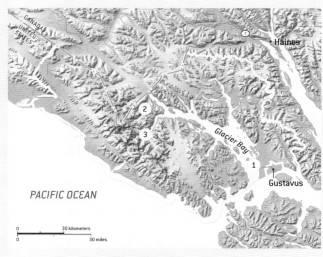

GLACIER BAY ALASKA

AREA
3,283,000 acres (13,286 sq km)

ESTABLISHED
December 1980

VISITOR INFORMATION
(907) 697 2230;
www.nps.gov/glba

KEY ATTRACTIONS ① Bartlett Cove ② Margerie Glacier ③ Johns Hopkins Glacier

NOTABLE WILDLIFE Humpback whale, orca, brown (grizzly) bear, black bear, gray wolf, moose, Steller's sea lion, sea otter

Chunks of ice litter the shore of Glacier Bay below McBride Glacier, near the northern end of Muir Inlet. The national park and preserve encompasses over 50 named glaciers, most of which have been in continuous retreat for more than two centuries. A few glaciers on the bay's western side are advancing.

Glaciers whose "feet" reach to the sea are called tidewater glaciers. Visitors taking boat tours around Glacier Bay hope to see the spectacle of "calving," when a large section of ice breaks away and falls into the water. Here, Margerie Glacier calves new icebergs into the bay with an enormous splash.

Park rangers board ships as they enter the bay, providing commentary and answering passengers' questions. In fact, cruise ships account for the majority of visitors to Glacier Bay National Park and Preserve, which can be reached only by boat or airplane. A 10-mile road runs to the park from the small community of Gustavus, but no road leads to Gustavus from the outside world.

The park's visitor center and campground are located at Bartlett Cove, on the east side of Glacier Bay, near its mouth. Because of the park's topography, hiking trails are limited, but marked routes in the Bartlett Cove area allow exploration of the spruce-hemlock forest, the Bartlett River estuary, and Bartlett Lake, where loons call and moose may

wade into the water to feed and escape insects. Park rangers lead daily walks on the one-mile Forest Loop, helping visitors learn the plants and animals of this habitat. Another trail leads several miles along the coast of Glacier Bay to its mouth at Icy Strait. Walking this route can provide looks at seabirds and marine mammals.

One of the most rewarding ways to experience Glacier Bay is by sea kayak, either as part of a guided tour or independently. Kayaking allows boaters to travel in silence and solitude, to observe wildlife inconspicuously, and to find places to camp far from other visitors. Kayakers can leave from Bartlett Cove or can take the daily tour boat and be dropped off at locations around the bay. While this can

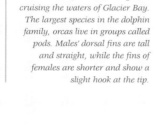

Orcas, also known as killer whales, are commonly seen cruising the waters of Glacier Bay. The largest species in the dolphin family, orcas live in groups called pods. Males' dorsal fins are tall and straight, while the fins of females are shorter and show a slight hook at the tip.

The boat passes near South Marble Island, where hundreds of sea lions may be resting on the shore. Great numbers of seabirds nest on this small island about 15 miles north of Bartlett Cove, including beautiful horned and tufted puffins. The island is also home to an important colony of pigeon guillemots, black birds with distinctive white upper wing patches. Bears and wolves roam the shoreline, while mountain goats walk along cliffs high above.

Passengers may thrill to the sight of humpback whales alongside the boat, "blowing" their breath spray high into the air or raising their tails above the surface of the water before diving. Pods of orcas, or killer whales (the largest species in the dolphin family), may appear in the bay, their tall dorsal fins making them conspicuous.

Glacier Bay National Park and Preserve encompasses more than 50 glaciers large enough to have been named, and these massive rivers of ice cover 1,375 square miles (27 percent) of the park. Seven of the glaciers are classified as tidewater, meaning their "feet" stretch into the water of the bay. Cruise boats pause near some of these glaciers to allow passengers the chance to observe "calving." With a loud crack like artillery fire, a chunk of ice breaks away from the main body of the glacier, dropping into the bay with (if it is big enough) a tremendous splash. Although calving is impossible to predict, it happens often enough that many park visitors experience this awesome natural event.

be a fantastic experience, kayakers need to understand rules for traveling in bear country (both black and brown bears are common in the park) and be cautious of riptides and other boating hazards. Tides in Glacier Bay can rise or fall as much as 23 feet within a six-hour period.

For many Glacier Bay visitors, the best way to see the park's landscape is to take the authorized commercial tour boat, which leaves Bartlett Cove each morning in summer for a seven-hour trip around the farthest reaches of the bay. Following a 130-mile loop, this cruise has a National Park Service ranger on board to discuss geology and history and help spot wildlife. Travelers on the boat should pack clothing appropriate for the notoriously changeable Alaska weather.

The tufted puffin is one of many species of seabirds, including gulls, guillemots, and cormorants, that nest on rocky islands and cliffs around Glacier Bay. Tufted puffins feed on small fish, squid, and krill. When young leave the nest, they may remain far out to sea for years before returning to their breeding colony.

WRANGELL-ST. ELIAS NATIONAL PARK AND PRESERVE

NAMED FOR TWO RANGES OF SPECTACULAR mountains, Wrangell-St. Elias ranks as the largest national park in the United States. More than half the size of the state of Virginia, this vast park is a place of perpetually snow-capped peaks, icy rivers, abundant wildlife, and a wilderness area nearly twice the size of New Jersey.

More than a quarter of the park is covered by glaciers, including several notable for their enormous size. Nabesna Glacier, more than 75 miles long, is the world's longest interior valley glacier, while Malaspina Glacier, at around 1,500 square miles, is North America's largest piedmont glacier (a glacier that has flowed out onto flat land at the foot of a valley), covering an area larger than the state of Rhode Island. The Bagley Icefield, 127 miles long and 6 miles wide (North America's largest subpolar icefield), feeds dozens of glaciers that travel down slopes from its circumference.

It is the park's mountains that draw the visitor's eye, though: awesome peaks almost beyond numbering, so many that only a tiny fraction of them can be seen from any single viewpoint. The park includes parts of four mountain ranges: Wrangell, St. Elias, Chugach, and Alaska. Nine of the 16 highest peaks in the United States rise within the park, including Mt. St. Elias—at 18,008 feet the second-highest mountain in the country. Mt. St. Elias is located in a remote area on the border with Canada's Yukon Territory, but several of the park's most dramatic summits can be seen from roads around or in the park.

Wrangell-St. Elias National Park and Preserve forms a contiguous tract with two Canadian national parks, Kluane and Tatshenshini-Alsek, and America's Glacier Bay National Park,

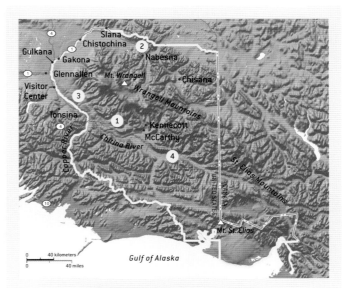

WRANGELL-ST. ELIAS ALASKA

AREA
13,175,795 acres (53,321 sq km)

ESTABLISHED
December 1980

VISITOR INFORMATION
(907) 822 5234;
www.nps.gov/wrst

KEY ATTRACTIONS ① McCarthy
Road ② Nabesna Road
③ Copper River ④ Chitina River

NOTABLE WILDLIFE Grizzly bear,
black bear, gray wolf, caribou,
Dall sheep, mountain goat,
moose, trumpeter swan

The massive and rugged St. Elias Mountains rise near the Gulf of Alaska, stretching across both the United States and Canada. The 18,008-foot summit of Mount St. Elias is located on the border of Alaska and Yukon Territory, so is considered the second-highest peak in both countries.

Glaciers cover more than one-fourth of the national park and preserve, an area of around 5,000 square miles. At 76 miles long, Hubbard Glacier, seen here, is North America's largest tidewater glacier. It is one of the few Alaskan glaciers advancing despite the warming global climate.

which taken together have been designated a World Heritage Site. The four parks compose the world's largest international protected wilderness.

The Wrangell Mountains comprise an extensive volcanic landscape, where during the past 5 million years volcanoes have erupted thousands of times, depositing vast amounts of lava over the Earth. The heat that fuels this activity comes from the collision of the Pacific and North American tectonic plates deep beneath the surface, part of the "Ring of Fire" of seismic and volcanic activity stretching from New Zealand to Chile. The only still-active volcano in the park is Mount Wrangell, which last erupted in 1900. Steam can be seen venting from the crater atop 14,163-foot Wrangell, which by volume is one of the world's largest active volcanoes.

Wrangell-St. Elias protects an excellent array of Alaska's legendary wildlife. Grizzly and black bears, caribou, moose, and reintroduced bison feed in the tundra and foothills, while Dall sheep and mountain goats wander the higher elevations. Packs of gray wolves roam the park, part of the natural balance

With a range primarily confined to far northern forests, the great gray owl is found in North America, Europe, and Asia. It appears much more massive than its true body size because of dense feathers that help it survive cold winters. This female holds a vole brought to her on the nest by her mate.

of predator and prey. Anglers seek sport fish that abound in the park's broad, braided rivers, including salmon, trout, and grayling.

Only two roads enter the park's interior, both offering fantastic opportunities to admire breathtaking scenery and observe wildlife. The 61-mile gravel McCarthy Road heads east from the village of Chitina along an old railroad corridor, with snow-capped 12,010-foot Mount Drum looming to the north. Along the way the road crosses the Kuskulana River on a one-lane bridge, a former railroad trestle, 238 feet above the rushing water. Wolves, lynx, and bald eagles might be seen feeding on the salmon that congregate at Long Lake. The road ends at the Kennicott River, flowing from beneath a glacier, and the old copper-mining community of McCarthy, with the restored mine buildings of the Kennecott National Historic Landmark district 5 miles away (reached on foot or by shuttle).

The park's other vehicle entry point, 42-mile Nabesna Road, winds through scrubby woodland and shrubs, surrounded by peaks of the Wrangell, Mentasta, and Nutzotin Mountains. Even more primitive than the McCarthy Road, the Nabesna Road has very limited services; drivers should check with park rangers before beginning travel. (Good spare tires are essential on both park roads.) To the south rises 16,237-foot Mount Sanford. Moose, Dall sheep, and grizzly bears might be seen along the road, which ends at a gold mine that still operates as a private enterprise.

There are many ways to see Wrangell-St. Elias National Park and Preserve other than from vehicles. Rafting is popular on several park rivers, which flow strongly in summer with water from melting snow and glaciers. Local outfitters can provide guide services for river rafting or backcountry hiking, which often involves transportation to remote locations by airplane. Bush pilots also deliver skiers to park glaciers and icefields for wilderness trips combining skiing and camping. For those who want spectacular high-elevation views of the park, scenic flights are offered from several adjacent communities. Only from the air is it possible to get a visual sense of just how huge are the park and its mountains and glaciers, range after range disappearing to the horizon, most of it never experiencing a human footprint.

Wrangell-St. Elias is so immense that first-time visitors should seek advice on the best ways to experience its many qualities. An excellent visitor center, located at Mile 106 of the Richardson Highway, is the best starting point for adventures. Besides exhibits, a film, and ranger-led hikes, the center offers the chance to walk an original section of the Valdez Trail, a historic route from the Gulf of Alaska to the interior used by pioneer miners and settlers. The expansive tract of wild Alaska within Wrangell-St. Elias National Park and Preserve is in many ways little changed from the wilderness experienced by those travelers.

KENAI FJORDS NATIONAL PARK

THE DRAMATIC LANDSCAPE OF KENAI Fjords National Park owes its rugged beauty to ice. On this spectacular section of the Gulf of Alaska coastline, dozens of glaciers have pushed down to the sea, carving deep valleys that later were partially submerged by saltwater. It was in part to preserve the pristine qualities of these fjords along the east side of Alaska's Kenai Peninsula that the national park was created.

The park also protects the enormous Harding Icefield, the most expansive icefield found entirely within the United States. Stretching across more than 300 square miles, this virtual ocean of ice is the source of at least 38 glaciers. As much as 60 feet of snow falls on the icefield each year, compressing the snow below into ice that continually feeds the "rivers of ice" that are glaciers. Appearing above the Harding Icefield, like islands in a white sea, are the isolated ice-free tops of mountains called nunataks (from the Inuit "nunataq").

The nature of the park's terrain, along with the extent of permanent ice, means that very little of its interior is accessible except to experienced and properly prepared mountaineers. The only part of Kenai Fjords reachable by road is the Exit Glacier area, a few miles north of the town of Seward, where the park visitor center is located.

Exit Glacier is reached by a paved, 8.6-mile road leading up the Resurrection River Valley. Signs along the road indicate how far the glacier has retreated over the past decades. Like almost all park glaciers, Exit has been steadily shrinking, exposing land that has been buried under hundreds of feet of ice for thousands of years. A nature center here is

KENAI FJORDS ALASKA

AREA
669,982 acres (2,711 sq km)

ESTABLISHED
December 1980

VISITOR INFORMATION
(907) 224 7500;
www.nps.gov/kefj

KEY ATTRACTIONS ① Exit Glacier
② Harding Icefield

NOTABLE WILDLIFE Humpback whale, orca, sea otter, Dall's porpoise, Steller's sea lion, black bear

Steller's sea lions are among the many species of marine mammals that might be seen during a boat tour of Resurrection Bay and the Gulf of Alaska, along with sea otters, Dall's porpoises, orcas (killer whales), gray whales, and humpback whales. Park rangers accompany many tours.

open in summer, and hiking trails allow close views of the beautiful blue ice of Exit Glacier and distant views of Harding Icefield.

Many people enjoy exploring the coast of the Kenai Peninsula by sea kayak, paddling along striking cliffs and into fjords. Sudden storms and rough water can make such a trip dangerous, though: the safest way to enjoy kayaking is via guided trip. Floatplanes or water taxis can transport park visitors and their kayaks and supplies to remote areas for camping trips, where the meeting of rocky shore and sea provides the solitude of true wilderness.

The most popular way to enjoy the park's coastline takes advantage of one of the many companies offering boat tours from Seward. Full-day tours travel to "tidewater" glaciers (those that extend to the sea) and pass islands where sea lions, seals, and tremendous numbers of seabirds can be seen. In addition, chances are good for spotting marine mammals such as humpback whales, orcas (killer whales), and porpoises. Those tours, some of which feature National Park Service rangers providing narration, allow visitors to experience the best of the park, from its wondrous fjords to its diverse and abundant wildlife.

The immense Harding Icefield is the source of at least 38 glaciers, the largest of which is Bear Glacier (above). The glacier descends 5,000 feet into Bear Glacier Lake, where giant icebergs—some over 100 feet high—frequently split off, or "calve," into the water. Bear Glacier is currently retreating rapidly.

KATMAI NATIONAL PARK AND PRESERVE

BIOLOGISTS ESTIMATE THAT MORE THAN 2,000 brown bears live in this vast park in southwestern Alaska, making it an important population center for the species that is the largest land predator in North America. In summer, brown bears (the coastal form of grizzly bear) gather along streams to feed on abundant salmon, creating one of the world's most awe-inspiring wildlife-watching opportunities. Katmai National Park and Preserve can be reached only by floatplane or boat; no roads lead into the park. Weather can make access unpredictable at times, but for those who undertake the journey, the memories will last a lifetime.

The center of park activity is Brooks Camp, located where the Brooks River flows into Naknek Lake, one of several lakes in the region created when glacial deposits formed dams in valleys. Here, a series of rapids on the river attract a staggering concentration of bears in July and September. Visitors gather on viewing platforms to photograph the spectacle, getting breathtakingly intimate looks while allowing the bears to pursue their natural activities. The presence of so many huge bears—males, gorging on fat-rich salmon, can weigh up to 2,100 pounds—means that all visitors must attend a safety program on arrival, and there are strict rules about food storage and other activities in camp.

Katmai was originally declared a national monument in 1918 to protect geological features associated with the 1912 eruption of the Novarupta volcano, a blast of such violence that it could be heard in Juneau, 750 miles away. More than 6 cubic miles of ash were ejected by the eruption, one of the five largest ever recorded.

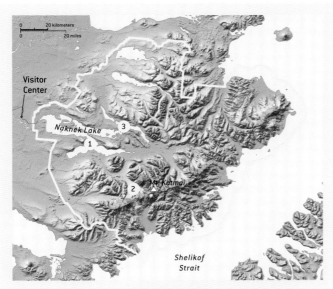

KATMAI ALASKA

AREA
4,700,000 acres (19,020 sq km)
ESTABLISHED
December 1980
VISITOR INFORMATION
(907) 246 3305;
www.nps.gov/katm

KEY ATTRACTIONS ① Brooks Camp ② Valley of Ten Thousand Smokes ③ Savonoski Loop
NOTABLE WILDLIFE Brown bear, gray wolf, moose, caribou, lynx, wolverine

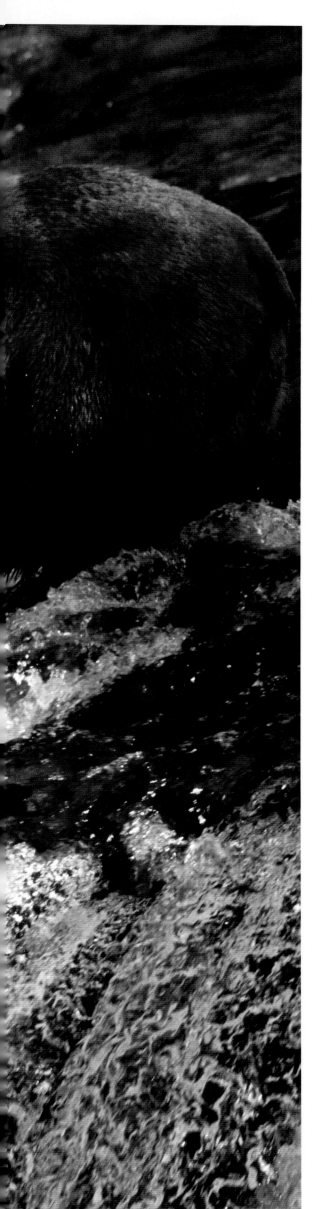

A geologist who visited the area later called one site the "Valley of Ten Thousand Smokes," and it was this phenomenon that inspired the park's establishment.

While most of those geothermal features have since cooled, Katmai still encompasses several active volcanoes, and volcanic and seismic events are common. In summer, park rangers lead daily bus trips from Brooks Camp to the Valley of Ten Thousand Smokes, allowing visitors to experience the stark landscape created by the Novarupta explosion. Adventurous and well-prepared hikers can set off from the valley to explore locations associated with the eruption, traversing a terrain deeply covered in ash and eroded into countless stream-cut ravines.

Among the other popular activities at Katmai is the Savonoski Loop, an 86-mile wilderness trip for canoeists and kayakers.

Requiring five to ten days, this route provides an unsurpassed experience in Alaska's backcountry, as paddlers traverse lakes and rivers through habitats that are home to bears, wolves, moose, and caribou.

Beyond Brooks Camp and the Valley of Ten Thousand Smokes lies a park of more than 7,300 square miles, most of it rarely touched by human footprints. While hikers are free to roam this wild landscape, backcountry experience and planning are essential. Storms can form quickly at any season, making rivers unfordable, disrupting schedules, and delaying transportation plans. The reward for careful preparation is one of the continent's most striking landscapes, where smoking volcanic peaks loom above lakes and winding rivers, and natural processes endure as they have for millennia.

Mount Katmai's 6,715-foot summit rises above the Valley of Ten Thousand Smokes, an area of 40 square miles covered in ash deposits hundreds of feet deep from the massive 1912 Novarupta volcanic eruption. Park rangers lead seasonal bus tours to an observation point overlooking the valley.

LAKE CLARK NATIONAL PARK AND PRESERVE

Mount Redoubt has in recent times been one of Alaska's most active volcanoes, pouring lava and ash from its 10,197-foot summit. Like other volcanoes in the state, Redoubt is part of the Pacific "Ring of Fire" seismic zone, which arcs from New Zealand north to Alaska and back south to Chile.

ENCOMPASSING MORE THAN 4 MILLION acres on the northern part of the Alaska Peninsula, Lake Clark National Park and Preserve offers travelers a compendium of distinctive wilderness environments typical of the country's largest state. Rugged, rocky coast; broad, braided rivers fed by glaciers; vast lakes; imposing mountain ranges; active volcanoes; spruce forests; immense tracts of grassland and tundra where bears, wolves, and caribou roam—all these habitats can be found within Lake Clark.

No roads exist within the park; access is provided by the charter airplanes and air taxi services that are ubiquitous in the Alaskan backcountry. Floatplanes land on lakes, while wheeled planes land on river gravel bars or primitive airstrips. A small visitor center is located in the village of Port Alsworth, on the southern shore of Lake Clark, but the great majority of the park consists of wilderness with no campgrounds, trails, or other development.

The most popular activities in the park are fishing (for abundant species such as arctic grayling, salmon, and lake trout), hunting (allowed in the preserve section of the combined park and preserve), and rafting on the park's rivers, several of which have been officially designated as federal Wild and Scenic Rivers. Private lodges exist in the

LAKE CLARK ALASKA

AREA
4,030,000 acres (16,309 sq km)

ESTABLISHED
December 1980

VISITOR INFORMATION
(907) 781 2218;
www.nps.gov/lacl

KEY ATTRACTIONS ① Lake Clark
② Telaquana Trail ③ Mulchatna
④ Chilikadrotna ⑤ Tlikakila

NOTABLE WILDLIFE Grizzly
and black bears, caribou,
moose, Dall sheep, gray wolf,
trumpeter swan

A solitary canoeist paddles on Turquoise Lake (Vandaztun Vena in the Dena'ina Athabascan language) in the western part of Lake Clark National Park and Preserve. The lake derives its rich color from tiny particles of glacial "powder" carried by rivers from high up in the surrounding mountains.

park catering to outdoorspeople, and many guide services offer river trips that range in duration from a few days to a week or more.

Although there are stretches of whitewater with Class III and IV rapids, most rivers in Lake Clark National Park and Preserve are swiftly flowing flatwater. Depending on the trip, boaters may pass through broad valleys with tundra and sparse forest, or along dramatic canyons under glaciers. Moose and black and grizzly bears might appear on river banks.

Hikers may wander anywhere in this huge park, but unpredictable weather, the lack of maintained trails, and difficulty in contacting rescue services mean the Lake Clark backcountry is best suited for experienced wilderness travelers. Nature in Lake Clark is wild and uncompromising, the qualities that make Alaska itself so appealing to adventurous travelers. Many backpackers enjoy the challenge of the 50-mile Telaquana Trail, a historic route long used by the Dena'ina Athabascan people as well as by miners and fur trappers. Hikers on this primitive route must cross high mountain passes, ford rivers, and in places find their own way across the heart of the park.

Lake Clark National Park and Preserve is noted for its active volcanoes—two inside the park and two others just outside its boundaries—which have erupted frequently over the past decades. In March, 2009, the park's Mount Redoubt came to life, with several explosions sending ash and gas clouds more than 60,000 feet into the air and creating a lava flow more than a half-mile long. Mount Redoubt has erupted five times since 1900 and is expected to continue its activity.

Ruth Glacier flows to the south of Mount McKinley, part of the huge glacial system that covers more than a million acres of Denali National Park and Preserve. McKinley is rising at about a millimeter each year, a result of tectonic forces far below the Earth's surface creating uplift in the Alaska Range.

DENALI NATIONAL PARK AND PRESERVE

THE CENTERPIECE OF THIS HUGE wilderness park is of course the highest mountain in North America, the 20,320-foot summit called both Mount McKinley and Denali—the latter its name in the local Athabascan language (meaning "the high one"). On days when the weather clears, the massive peak dominates the landscape, its rugged, snow-capped profile one of the icons of Alaska.

Yet it was to conserve wildlife, rather than to enshrine the mountain, that the original national park was established here in 1917. A gold rush occurring right after the start of the 20th century had led to an influx of miners, who were killing wildlife at an unsustainable level. It was not until decades later that the entire mountain was included within the park boundaries. Today, visitors enjoy stunning panoramas of the Alaska Range mountains and vast expanses of tundra, but also treasure the park for opportunities to see bears, moose, Dall sheep, caribou, and gray wolves.

Glaciers largely retreated from this landscape about 10,000 years ago, yet their remnants endure high in the Alaska Range, where brief summers do not melt permanent tracts of ice. Below lie immense areas of tundra with scattered woodlands of spruce, aspen, and birch and dense thickets of willow and alder. Shallow, braided rivers are fed by snowmelt, and countless lakes dot the terrain. Rugged, rocky hills lie along the sides of broad valleys. All of these elements create a park of breathtaking beauty as well as ecological riches.

Only a single road winds into the heart of Denali National Park and Preserve, a 91-mile mostly gravel route from the visitor center area on the park's eastern border to the old mining town

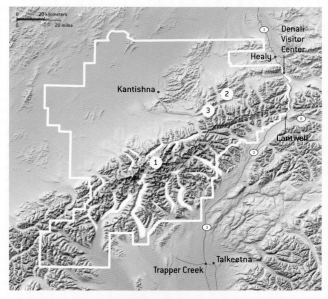

DENALI ALASKA

AREA
6,075,028 acres (24,585 sq km)
ESTABLISHED
February 1917
VISITOR INFORMATION
(907) 683 2294;
www.nps.gov/dena

KEY ATTRACTIONS ① Mount McKinley ② Polychrome Pass ③ Eielson Visitor Center
NOTABLE WILDLIFE Grizzly bear, black bear, gray wolf, caribou, Dall sheep, moose, gyrfalcon

The highest point in North America, 20,320-foot Mount McKinley dominates the landscape for miles in all directions. Its alternative name, Denali, means "the high one" in the native Athabascan language. The caribou is one of many species of wildlife that attract visitors to this 6 million-acre park.

of Kantishna. To protect the park's environment, and to give travelers a more peaceful experience, private vehicles are allowed only on the first 15 miles of the road. Beyond that, a system of shuttle buses allows visitors to ride to various destinations along the road, or to take all-day guided tours with interpreters pointing out wildlife and explaining geology.

Although visitors are eager to see Denali's interior, the park's entrance area includes several worthwhile attractions. The main visitor center offers an excellent introductory film, exhibits, and information on the many ranger-led hikes and programs. The park's sled dogs are housed in a kennel near the entrance, where rangers hold demonstrations daily in summer. Most of Denali's maintained hiking trails are found near the entrance, providing access to wetlands good for wildlife-spotting, taiga (boreal forest), and high-elevation viewpoints with stunning panoramas.

Visitors taking a bus trip into the park might, on a clear day, spot Mount McKinley around mile 9 of the main road. After passing through taiga, the route enters an expanse of tundra, where moose, caribou, and gray wolves often appear nearby. The park is home to both black and grizzly bears. From the road,

most bears seen are grizzlies, which prefer open areas; black bears tend to remain in forests. Much of the park terrain is underlain by permafrost, or permanently frozen earth just below the surface. This limits plant growth to herbs, grasses, shrubs, and small trees. The "drunken forest" seen from the park road results from the temporary melting of permafrost, causing land slips that tilt trees at odd angles.

The road hugs hillsides through Polychrome Pass, where an overlook offers wonderful panoramic views of the Alaska Range, tundra, and braided rivers. Dall sheep, a relative of the bighorn sheep found farther south, can often be seen grazing on steep mountain slopes high above the road.

After crossing the Toklat River, the park road arrives at the Eielson Visitor Center, rebuilt in 2008 as a showcase of environmentally friendly sustainable design. In this often rainy climate, Mount McKinley can be seen to the southwest, more than 40 miles away, on about one day of every three. When the peak does show itself, the vista is among the finest in Alaska. Although many mountains around the world are taller than McKinley in summit height above sea level, few rival it in its rise from the surrounding landscape. McKinley stands about

The gyrfalcon is the largest and most powerful of all the falcons. Its highly variable plumage can range from almost pure white to dark brown; females are noticeably larger than males. Ptarmigans make up more than half the gyrfalcon's diet.

An estimated 90–100 gray wolves roam Denali in around 14 packs, each with an "alpha pair" of adults, along with their young and non-breeding adults. Each pack ranges over its home territory in search of prey, traveling up to 30 miles in a day. Their howl is heard most often in evening and early morning.

18,000 feet higher than the lowlands around it, whereas Mount Everest, the planet's highest mountain, is about 12,000 feet above its supporting plateau.

Nineteen miles ahead is the side road to the Wonder Lake campground. A trailhead here provides access to the 4.5-mile round-trip McKinley Bar Trail, one of the few developed trails away from the park entrance area. This easy walk leads through spruce forest and tundra to reach the McKinley River and the gravel bars typical of shallow, many channeled streams. Wildlife from caribou to bears might be seen here.

Many visitors look forward to a backpacking trip through Denali's wilderness, enjoying the beauty and solitude of one of the continent's most pristine landscapes. Rough terrain, unpredictable weather, and the presence of bears mean careful preparation is required, but for experienced hikers Denali provides a fantastic opportunity to explore the subarctic environment. A less demanding way to see the park's backcountry is to take a ranger-led Discovery Hike. These three- to five-hour treks, ranging from moderate to strenuous in physical demand, allow a maximum of 11 participants to accompany a park ranger into wild places away from roads.

GATES OF THE ARCTIC NATIONAL PARK AND PRESERVE

BACKPACKERS IN GATES OF THE ARCTIC National Park and Preserve can find themselves as far from civilization as anywhere within America's national park system. Spreading across more than 13,000 square miles and located entirely north of the Arctic Circle, this wilderness park has no roads, developed trails, campgrounds, or other services, except for a small village of the native Nunamiut people incorporated within the northern part of the park.

Mountains of the vast and little-traveled Brooks Range make up much of the park, rugged summits creating a formidable barrier to travel. Many park visitors are dropped off by airplane to raft one of six designated Wild and Scenic Rivers that flow in part through Gates of the Arctic. It was a scene along one of these streams that inspired the park's name.

In the 1930s, famed wilderness advocate Bob Marshall was traveling through the region when he came across two peaks flanking a stretch of the North Fork of the Koyukuk River, creating a figurative portal. He called this spot "Gates of the Arctic," a name that was applied when the area was made a national monument in 1978 and a national park two years later.

Flowing down from the spectacular high country of the Brooks Range, some park rivers follow the U-shaped valleys typical of glacial carving, while others run through steep-sided V-shaped canyons cut by the rivers themselves. Stretching in a near-endless expanse all around is a tundra landscape that is home to grizzly bears, gray wolves, muskoxen, and caribou.

Spruce forests blanket some areas of the south slope of the Brooks Range, creating additional habitat for diverse wildlife.

Most of those who enter Gates of the Arctic on foot do so from the village of Anaktuvuk Pass or from the Dalton Highway, which runs near the park's eastern edge. Hikes of any length are possible, though travel through this wild and remote region necessitates excellent backcountry skills, including route-finding ability and bear-country precautions. Summers are brief this far north, and freezing temperatures and snow are possibilities even in midsummer. Those who arrange for airplane transportation must be prepared for delays of several days if storms set in.

Gates of the Arctic is not a park for everyone, but for those who have the time and skills to explore its wild reaches, it represents one of the last spots in the United States truly untouched by human activities, where wildlife exists in the same cycles of nature that have ruled the Arctic for thousands of years.

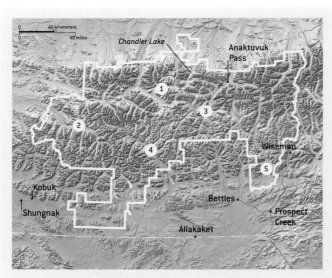

GATES OF THE ARCTIC ALASKA

AREA
8,472,500 acres (34,287 sq km)
ESTABLISHED
December 1980
VISITOR INFORMATION
(907) 692 5494;
www.nps.gov/gaar

KEY ATTRACTIONS ① Brooks Range ② Noatak River ③ John River ④ Alatna River ⑤ North Fork of the Koyukuk
NOTABLE WILDLIFE Grizzly bear, muskox, gray wolf, caribou, Dall sheep

Muskoxen disappeared from Alaska in the mid-19th century as a result of uncontrolled hunting. Reintroduced beginning in the 1930s, they have increased to around 4,000 individuals. The species is named for the strong odor emitted by males during the mating season.

Fireweed blooms near the 5,501-foot peak called Frigid Crags, which rises alongside the North Fork of the Koyukuk River. Wilderness advocate Bob Marshall named Gates of the Arctic for this mountain and 6,654-foot Boreal Mountain, which together form a "gate" on opposite sides of the river.

KOBUK VALLEY
NATIONAL PARK

I N SOME YEARS, KOBUK VALLEY IS THE LEAST-visited national park within the National Park Service system, with only about 1,000 travelers entering its boundaries. This is a testament to its remote location within the sparsely settled state of Alaska, above the Arctic Circle, with no roads in or even near the park. What this means for those who do visit is the assurance of an experience of great solitude, exploring a wildlife-rich river, an expansive swath of tundra, and the oddity of a tract of sand dunes located in the Arctic.

The 350-mile-long Kobuk River begins as a whitewater stream in Gates of the Arctic National Park, leaving the mountains to become a broad, slow-moving river as it passes for 61 miles through Kobuk Valley National Park. (Kobuk is an Inupiaq Inuit word meaning "big river.") The wide river valley is a major migration route for caribou, with nearly half a million of these animals (the largest herd in Alaska) passing through the region twice annually. Archeologists have found evidence that native people have gathered at a spot on the river bank called Onion Portage in fall for more than 9,000 years to hunt caribou for winter sustenance.

Most park visitors arrive by air taxi during the very brief summer season, being dropped off upstream from the park and floating down the Kobuk River, stopping often to fish, hike, and sightsee. In places the river banks are made up of bluffs 150 feet tall, some with fossils of mammals dating to the most recent ice age.

On the south bank of the river, the park protects three areas of sand dunes, together composing a 25-square-mile expanse. Some of the dunes rise as much as 100 feet tall. This seemingly incongruous landscape was created over thousands of years by

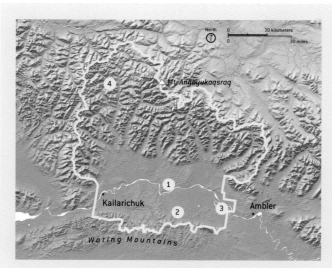

KOBUK VALLEY ALASKA

AREA
1,750,700 acres (7,085 sq km)
ESTABLISHED
December 1980
VISITOR INFORMATION
(907) 442 3890;
www.nps.gov/kova

KEY ATTRACTIONS ① Kobuk River ② Great Kobuk Sand Dunes ③ Onion Portage ④ Baird Mountains
NOTABLE WILDLIFE Grizzly bear, black bear, caribou, muskox, gray wolf

glacial action (grinding bedrock into sand) and prevailing winds. The dune field, the largest active expanse of dunes north of the Arctic Circle, is continually reshaped by winds, preventing plants from intruding. Despite its far-north geographic location, the dune field sometimes sees summer temperatures of more than 100 degrees.

Hikers find that walking across the tundra can be a tiring slog, with the ground remaining soggy all year because underlying permafrost (frozen earth) does not allow water to drain away. Those who explore Kobuk Valley by foot try to hike along ridgetops when possible. Grizzly bears are common in the park, and backpackers should obey rules about cooking sites and food storage to prevent unwanted campsite visitors.

The taiga (the northern portion of the boreal forest) reaches its limit in the park, with scattered small spruce trees surviving long, severe winter conditions. Although snow covers the ground for most of the year and the Kobuk River is ice-bound for an equally long period, summer brings an explosion of life to the park, as migratory birds return, mammals give birth to young, and colorful wildflowers carpet the tundra. Biologists estimate that around 400 species of plants, 120 birds, 32 mammals, and one amphibian (the wood frog) make their homes in the park.

Kobuk Valley National Park is managed in cooperation with the local Inupiaq Inuit community, members of which have been allowed to continue hunting and trapping for subsistence harvest within the park even after it was established in 1980. Visitors may come across sites associated with native cultures, both historic and contemporary. Campsites and lodges should not be disturbed, and hikers who come across archeological sites are asked to report their locations to park rangers.

The first snow of fall dusts distant mountain slopes as caribou swim across the Kobuk River on their southbound migration. Nearly a half-million caribou pass through the Kobuk Valley twice annually as they move between summer and winter feeding and calving areas.

In continuous eruption since 1983, vents in Hawaii Volcanoes National Park expel lava that flows downhill to meet the Pacific Ocean in a spectacular display of fire and steam. Having destroyed dozens of buildings, the lava flows have also added more than 570 acres of land to the "Big Island" of Hawaii.

HAWAII VOLCANOES NATIONAL PARK

THE MOST GEOGRAPHICALLY ISOLATED island group on Earth, the Hawaiian Islands were formed during a period of 70 million years as the Pacific Ocean floor moved over a volcanic "hot spot." This site has erupted unimaginable amounts of lava, creating a chain of towering mountains that rise above the surface of the sea. The "Big Island" of Hawaii, the youngest and largest of the islands, is actually a conglomeration of five volcanoes, and is home to some of the most frequent and easily observable volcanic activity found anywhere in the world.

Hawaii Volcanoes National Park is the scene of much of this activity, comprising two major volcanoes, Mauna Loa and Kilauea. The former erupted most recently in 1984, while Kilauea has been erupting continuously since 1983, and came to life with renewed vigor when a new vent opened in Halemaumau Crater in March, 2008. The park showcases more than volcanoes, as well: Spanning an elevation range from the 13,677-foot summit of Mauna Loa to sea level, Hawaii Volcanoes National Park encompasses seven life zones with a correspondingly diverse array of plants and animals, including many endangered species.

The unpredictable nature of the park's volcanoes means that visitors must be prepared for changeable conditions, including temporary or long-term closure of some areas and facilities. During Kilauea's eight-year period of eruption beginning in 1983, more than 180 houses were destroyed, along with a park visitor center and other buildings. Hot lava continues to flow

HAWAII VOLCANOES ISLAND OF HAWAII

AREA
323,431 acres (1,309 sq km)

ESTABLISHED
August 1916

VISITOR INFORMATION
(808) 985 6000;
www.nps.gov/havo

KEY ATTRACTIONS ① Crater Rim Drive ② Chain of Craters Road ③ Kilauea caldera ④ Mauna Loa

NOTABLE WILDLIFE Nene, Hawaiian hawk, akepa, Hawaii creeper, omao, hawksbill turtle

Young tree ferns add color to a barren park landscape, cleared of earlier vegetation by lava flows and ash falls. With an elevation range of well over 2 miles, Hawaii Volcanoes National Park encompasses a broad diversity of plant and animal life, from rain forest to mountain peaks.

down to the Pacific, meeting the sea with accompanying clouds of steam. Cooled lava creates "benches" of new rock, dangerous to walk on because they can collapse into the ocean without warning. In addition, sulfur dioxide and other gases emitted from vents can create breathing problems if inhaled, and "vog" (volcanic fog) sometimes covers large areas in and around the park.

With proper precautions, visitors can enjoy a memorable visit, seeing landscapes created by volcanic activity and experiencing our planet in its youngest and rawest form. The visitor center offers exhibits and a film that explain the geology, and rangers can provide information on conditions. The 11-mile Crater Rim Drive makes a loop around the main Kilauea caldera, though the 2008 eruptions caused closure of the western section. The drive still provides access to viewpoints and trailheads, giving adventurous visitors the chance to see the volcanic terrain in detail.

The easy, 1-mile Devastation Trail, for example, leads into an area of forest destroyed by cinders from lava fountains of a 1959 eruption. This path allows observation of features such as Pele's hair (thread-thin rock material formed when lava flies through the air), olivine (a gem-like mineral), tree molds (impressions of trees in lava), cinder cones, and spatter cones. At the Thurston Lava Tube, visitors can walk through a 450-foot-long tunnel formed when the outside of a lava flow solidified and the molten middle emptied itself. At Sulphur Banks, the air smells of rotten eggs, from hydrogen sulfide fumes, and clay is stained red and brown, from iron oxide contained in vented gases. The nearby Steam Vents site shows the effects of groundwater meeting molten rock below the surface, boiling and rising as steam.

Anywhere along the drive, visitors may see nene, the native Hawaiian goose that is slowly recovering from near-

extinction. In areas of rain forest, brilliantly colored honeycreepers flit among the foliage. While a few species of these native birds remain common, some have become extinct and others are critically endangered from habitat loss, disease, and other factors. Hard to miss is the distinctive shape of the Mauna Loa silversword, an endangered plant with a dense cluster of long, pointed leaves. These species are examples of the high degree of endemism (life forms found nowhere else) in Hawaii.

Chain of Craters Road winds from Crater Rim Drive down to the Pacific Ocean, descending 3,700 feet in 20 miles to a site where lava flows have buried the road to a depth of more than 100 feet in places. There are more than a dozen overlooks along the way, providing breathtaking views of cliffs, lava fields, and seacoast. Hiking trails branch off from the road, leading to dramatic volcanic landscapes of lava flows and rain forests full of tree ferns. The Puu Loa area preserves petroglyphs (figures incised in rock) created by native Hawaiians, with more than 20,000 images.

Depending on current conditions, it may be possible to observe the spectacular scene of molten lava flowing into the sea, sending up clouds of steam. Park rangers can provide information about viewing sites, which may be more accessible from roads outside the park. Since Kilauea's most recent activity began in 1983, eruptions of lava have added more than 570 acres of land to the island of Hawaii and buried almost 9 miles of highway.

North of Crater Rim Drive, Mauna Loa Road winds up the flank of this huge volcano, which by volume is the most massive mountain on Earth. The one-lane paved road ends at an elevation of 6,662 feet, leaving a very strenuous hike to the summit for backpackers who are prepared for high altitudes, severe weather, and a constantly ascending trail.

Although many park visitors crave the thrill of approaching closely to a lava flow, safety requires extreme caution and viewing from a distance. Seemingly solid crust may break, plunging a hiker into hot rocks, and benches of hardened lava along the coast may collapse into the sea without warning.

One of the group of birds called Hawaiian honeycreepers, the 'i'iwi has a decurved bill adapted to feeding on nectar from flower blossoms. Its population has declined dramatically in recent years, in part because of habitat loss and diseases spread by introduced mosquitoes.

HALEAKALA
NATIONAL PARK

Hiking trails at Haleakala Crater provide access to an otherworldly landscape of cinder cones, ash fields, and lava flows. Although often called a crater, the gigantic depression at the mountain summit actually resulted from the erosion of a ridge between two adjacent valleys, not from volcanic action.

HALEAKALA NATIONAL PARK IS A PLACE of stark volcanic desert and lush tropical rain forest, where visitors can hike across a terrain of barren cinder cones one day and swim in gorgeous river pools surrounded by verdant vegetation the next. It is home to endangered species found nowhere else on Earth, as well as throngs of visitors who consider it one of the must-see destinations on the Hawaiian island of Maui.

Elevations in the park range from sea level to more than 10,000 feet, though most visitors spend time at the extremes of that span. The most popular activity is a trip up the steep, winding road to the Haleakala summit area, for a chance to see and perhaps hike through a landscape created by thousands of years of volcanic activity. Haleakala comprises a huge shield volcano (one built up by repeated lava flows into a broadened shape), part of the many volcanoes that have formed the island chain of Hawaii in the heart of the Pacific Ocean.

Past the main visitor center, located at an elevation of 7,000 feet, the road passes a series of overlooks with views of the Haleakala crater, a huge area of barren ash and cinders dotted with volcanic cones, in colors from gray to buff to reddish. Not a true crater, this area was formed when erosion wore away the ridge between two high-mountain valleys. The road reaches a dead end at the 10,023-foot summit, known in Hawaiian as Puuulaula.

More than 30 miles of trails are available for hiking in the summit area. Some, such as the popular Sliding Sands Trail, descend into the crater at various places and lead to sites such as the colorful Ka Luu o Ka Oo cinder cone. With a free permit, backpackers can camp at one of the park's two wilderness campsites. There are also three isolated wilderness cabins.

The nene, a small native Hawaiian goose, and Haleakala silversword, a striking plant with a rosette of leaves and a tall

PACIFIC OCEAN

Lahaina
Wailuku • Paia
Kihei
MAUI
Wailua

KAHOOLAWE

| 0 | 10 kilometers |
| 0 | 10 miles |

HALEAKALA ISLAND OF MAUI

AREA
33,230 acres (134 sq km)
ESTABLISHED
July 1961
VISITOR INFORMATION
(808) 572 4400;
www.nps.gov/hale

KEY ATTRACTIONS ① Haleakala
Crater ② Sliding Sands Trail
③ Kipahulu ④ Oheo Gulch
⑤ Waimoku Falls
NOTABLE WILDLIFE Nene,
akepa, Maui parrotbill, apapane,
'i'iwi

flower spike, may be seen in the summit area; both are highly er.dangered and strictly protected. Overnight campers in some parts of the park may hear the nocturnal cries of the uau (Hawaiian dark-rumped petrel), an endangered seabird that nests at the top of Haleakala.

At its other elevational extreme, Haleakala National Park ranges down to the Pacific Ocean coast at the Kipahulu area, where the main attraction is the 2-mile Pipiwai Trail. This route follows the stream that flows through famed Oheo Gulch, a picturesque place of dense bamboo, tree ferns, and other vegetation. Natural pools invite swimming, and at the end of the trail is beautiful Waimoku Falls, cascading down a cliff more than 400 feet high. The tallest waterfall on the island of Maui, it is a fitting reward for the moderately strenuous uphill hike. The national park area beyond the falls, Kipahulu Valley Biological Reserve, is closed to public entry in order to protect birds such as the rare Maui parrotbill, as well as other animals and plants.

Much evidence of the native Hawaiian culture can be found in the Kipahulu area, and park rangers conduct regular programs interpreting archeological resources. As is the case over most of Hawaii, the weather at Kipahulu can change quickly, with frequent rains nourishing the rainforest vegetation that gives the site its exotic appearance.

Found only in Hawaii, the distinctively shaped silversword is related to sunflowers. Living for several decades, the plant sends up a shoot of flowers that can rise to more than 8 feet before dying. Collecting, and browsing by introduced goats, almost eliminated the silversword from Maui. It is now strictly protected.

NATIONAL PARK OF AMERICAN SAMOA

ONE OF THE NEWEST NATIONAL PARKS, established in 1988, the National Park of American Samoa includes lush tropical forests, coral reefs teeming with colorful fish, and pristine sandy beaches, all located far from standard tourist itineraries.

American Samoa, a United States territory since 1899, comprises five small volcanic islands and two very small coral atolls, located in the southern Pacific Ocean south of the Equator. (The other islands of the Samoa Archipelago form the independent nation of Samoa.) In recognition of longstanding Samoan traditions dealing with land ownership, park lands are leased from local villages, and visitors are asked to learn and follow customs to show respect for Samoan culture.

The national park includes three units on four islands. The Tutuila Unit is on the island of the same name, which is also home to the major American Samoa city of Pago Pago. A 3.7-mile trail leads to the summit of 1,610-foot Mount Alava, and is excellent for spotting birds such as cardinal honeyeater, purple-capped fruit-dove, and Samoan starling. Vegetation thickly covers the rugged hills in this area, where the most

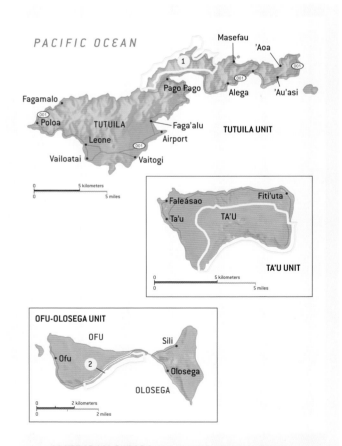

AMERICAN SAMOA ISLANDS OF AMERICAN SAMOA

AREA
13,500 acres (54 sq km)
ESTABLISHED
October 1988
VISITOR INFORMATION
(684) 633 7082;
www.nps.gov/npsa

KEY ATTRACTIONS ① Mount Alava
② Ofu Lagoon
NOTABLE WILDLIFE Samoan
fruit bat, white-naped fruit bat,
collared kingfisher, purple-capped
fruit-dove

conspicuous native mammals are two species of huge fruit bats (also called flying foxes), the Samoan fruit bat and the white-naped fruit bat, which are important pollinators of native flowers.

Also on Tutuila, two short trails lead to World War II sites, the Breakers Point and Blunt's Point gun emplacements. The park visitor center in Pago Pago can provide information on traveling to other park units.

The Ofu-Olosega Unit is located on two adjoining islands 60 miles east of Tutuila, reached by inter-island airplane flights. This area of the park is best known for picturesque beaches and coral reefs offering fine diving and snorkeling, especially in Ofu Lagoon. The kaleidoscope of fish species includes raccoon butterflyfish, pennant bannerfish, bullethead parrotfish, yellow-banded pipefish, and hundreds more.

The Ta'u Unit, also reached by air, features a coast trail to the island's southern shore with spectacular views of cliffs and beaches as well as 3,000-foot Lata Mountain.

National Park of American Samoa is a remote park with limited staffing and facilities, and one of its most attractive aspects is simply visiting villages and getting to know the Samoan people. A devastating tsunami that struck the islands in September 2009 destroyed the park offices and visitor center. Although natural features will recover, park activities will be curtailed for an undetermined time.

The masked booby is one of the many species of seabirds that can be seen breeding on the shores of American Samoa. It is a spectacular diver, plunging into the ocean to catch flying fish and other small fish. Although it is silent at sea, this booby's distinctive whistling greeting call can be heard at nesting colonies.

DIRECTORY OF PARKS

ACADIA NATIONAL PARK
P.O. Box 177
Bar Harbor, ME 04609
(207) 288 3338
www.nps.gov/acad

ARCHES NATIONAL PARK
P.O. Box 907
Moab, UT 84532
(435) 719 2299
www.nps.gov/arch

BADLANDS NATIONAL PARK
25216 Ben Reifel Road
P.O. Box 6
Interior, SD 57750
(605) 433 5361
www.nps.gov/badl

BIG BEND NATIONAL PARK
P.O. Box 129
Big Bend National Park, TX 79834
(432) 477 2251
www.nps.gov/bibe

BISCAYNE NATIONAL PARK
9700 SW 328 Street
Homestead, FL 33033
(305) 230 7275
www.nps.gov/bisc

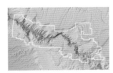

**BLACK CANYON OF THE GUNNISON
NATIONAL PARK**
102 Elk Creek
Gunnison, CO 81230
(970) 641 2337
www.nps.gov/blca

BRYCE CANYON NATIONAL PARK
P.O. Box 640201
Bryce, UT 84764
(435) 834 5322
www.nps.gov/brca

CANYONLANDS NATIONAL PARK
2282 SW Resource Boulevard
Moab, UT 84532
(435) 719 2313
Backcountry information
(435) 259 4351
www.nps.gov/cany

CAPITOL REEF NATIONAL PARK
HC 70 Box 15
Torrey, UT 84775
(435) 425 3791
www.nps.gov/care

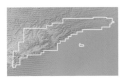

CARLSBAD CAVERNS NATIONAL PARK
3225 National Parks Highway
Carlsbad, NM 88220
(575) 785 2232
Bat flight information
(575) 785 3012
www.nps.gov/cave

CHANNEL ISLANDS NATIONAL PARK
1901 Spinnaker Drive
Ventura, CA 93001
(805) 658 5730
Outdoors Santa Barbara Visitor Center
113 Harbor Way 4th Floor
Santa Barbara, CA 93001
(805) 884 1475
www.nps.gov/chis

CONGAREE NATIONAL PARK
100 National Park Road
Hopkins, SC 29061
(803) 776 4396
www.nps.gov/cong

CRATER LAKE NATIONAL PARK
P.O. Box 7
Crater Lake, OR 97604
(541) 594 3000
www.nps.gov/crla

CUYAHOGA VALLEY NATIONAL PARK
15610 Vaughn Road
Brecksville, OH 44141
(216) 524 1497
(800) 445 9667
www.nps.gov/cuva

DEATH VALLEY NATIONAL PARK
P.O. Box 579
Death Valley, CA 92328
(760) 786 3200
www.nps.gov/deva

**DENALI NATIONAL PARK
AND PRESERVE**
P.O. Box 9
Denali Park, AK 99755
(907) 683 2294
Bus tour reservations
(800) 622 7275
www.nps.gov/dena

DRY TORTUGAS NATIONAL PARK
P.O. Box 6208
Key West, FL 33041
(305) 242 7700
www.nps.gov/drto

EVERGLADES NATIONAL PARK
40001 State Road 9336
Homestead, FL 33034
(305) 242 7700
www.nps.gov/ever

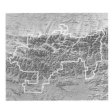

**GATES OF THE ARCTIC NATIONAL
PARK AND PRESERVE**
P.O. Box 30
Bettles, AK 99726
(907) 692 5494
www.nps.gov/gaar

**GLACIER BAY NATIONAL PARK
AND PRESERVE**
P.O. Box 140
Gustavus, AK 99826
(907) 697 2230
www.nps.gov/glba

GLACIER NATIONAL PARK
P.O. Box 128
West Glacier, MT 59936
(406) 888 7800
www.nps.gov/glac

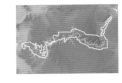

GRAND CANYON NATIONAL PARK
P.O. Box 129
Grand Canyon, AZ 86023
(928) 638 7888
www.nps.gov/grca

GRAND TETON NATIONAL PARK
P.O. Drawer 170
Moose, WY 83012
(307) 739 3300
www.nps.gov/grte

GREAT BASIN NATIONAL PARK
100 Great Basin National Park
Baker, NV 89311
(775) 234 7331
Lehman Caves advance tickets
(775) 234 7331 ext. 242
www.nps.gov/grba

**GREAT SAND DUNES NATIONAL
PARK AND PRESERVE**
11999 Highway 150
Mosca, CO 81146
(719) 378 6399
www.nps.gov/grsa

**GREAT SMOKY MOUNTAINS
NATIONAL PARK**
107 Park Headquarters Road
Gatlinburg, TN 37738
(865) 436 1200
www.nps.gov/grsm

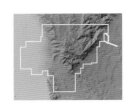

GUADALUPE MOUNTAINS NATIONAL PARK
400 Pine Canyon Road
Salt Flat, TX 79847
(915) 828 3251
www.nps.gov/gumo

HALEAKALA NATIONAL PARK
P.O. Box 369
Makawao, HI 96768
(808) 572 4400
www.nps.gov/hale

HAWAII VOLCANOES NATIONAL PARK
P.O. Box 52
Hawaii National Park, HI 96718
(808) 985 6000
www.nps.gov/havo

HOT SPRINGS NATIONAL PARK
101 Reserve Street
Hot Springs, AR 71901
(501) 624 2701
www.nps.gov/hosp

ISLE ROYALE NATIONAL PARK
800 East Lakeshore Drive
Houghton, MI 49931
(906) 482 0984
www.nps.gov/isro

JOSHUA TREE NATIONAL PARK
74485 National Park Drive
Twentynine Palms, CA 92277
(760) 367 5500
www.nps.gov/jotr

KATMAI NATIONAL PARK
AND PRESERVE
P.O. Box 7
King Salmon, AK 99613
(907) 246 3305
www.nps.gov/katm

KENAI FJORDS NATIONAL PARK
P.O. Box 1727
Seward, AK 99664
(907) 224 7500
www.nps.gov/kefj

KINGS CANYON NATIONAL PARK
47050 Generals Highway
Three Rivers, CA 93271
(559) 565 3341
www.nps.gov/seki

KOBUK VALLEY NATIONAL PARK
P.O. Box 1029
Kotzebue, AK 99752
(907) 442 3890
www.nps.gov/kova

LAKE CLARK NATIONAL PARK
AND PRESERVE
240 West 5th Avenue
Suite 236
Anchorage, AK 99501
(907) 644 3626
www.nps.gov/lacl

LASSEN VOLCANIC NATIONAL PARK
P.O. Box 100
Mineral, CA 96063
(530) 595 4480
www.nps.gov/lavo

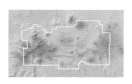
MAMMOTH CAVE NATIONAL PARK
1 Mammoth Cave Parkway
P.O. Box 7
Mammoth Cave, KY 42259
(270) 758 2180
Cave tour reservations
(877) 444 6777
www.nps.gov/maca
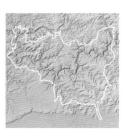

MESA VERDE NATIONAL PARK
P.O. Box 8
Mesa Verde, CO 81330
(970) 529 4465
www.nps.gov/meve

MOUNT RAINIER NATIONAL PARK
55210 238th Avenue East
Ashford, WA 98304
(360) 569 2211
www.nps.gov/mora

NATIONAL PARK OF AMERICAN SAMOA
Pago Pago, AS 96799-0001
(684) 633 7082
www.nps.gov/npsa

NORTH CASCADES
NATIONAL PARK
810 State Route 20
Sedro-Woolley, WA 98284
(360) 854 7200
www.nps.gov/noca

OLYMPIC NATIONAL PARK
600 East Park Avenue
Port Angeles, WA 98362
(360) 565 3130
www.nps.gov/olym

PETRIFIED FOREST NATIONAL PARK
P.O. Box 2217
Petrified Forest, AZ 86028
(928) 524 6228
www.nps.gov/pefo

REDWOOD NATIONAL AND
STATE PARKS
1111 Second Street
Crescent City, CA 95531
(707) 464 6101
www.nps.gov/redw

ROCKY MOUNTAIN NATIONAL PARK
1000 Highway 36
Estes Park, CO 80517
(970) 586 1206
www.nps.gov/romo

SAGUARO NATIONAL PARK
3693 South Old Spanish Trail
Tucson, AZ 85730
Rincon Mountain Visitor Center
(520) 733 5153
Tucson Mountain Visitor Center
(520) 733 5158
www.nps.gov/sagu

SEQUOIA NATIONAL PARK
47050 Generals Highway
Three Rivers, CA 93271
(559) 565 3341
www.nps.gov/seki

SHENANDOAH NATIONAL PARK
3655 US Highway 211 East
Luray, VA 22835
(540) 999 3500
www.nps.gov/shen

THEODORE ROOSEVELT
NATIONAL PARK
P.O. Box 7
Medora, ND 58645
South Unit Visitor Center
(701) 623 4730
North Unit Visitor Center
(701) 842 2333
www.nps.gov/thro

VIRGIN ISLANDS NATIONAL PARK
1300 Cruz Bay Creek
St. John, VI 00830
(340) 776 6201
www.nps.gov/viis

VOYAGEURS NATIONAL PARK
3131 Highway 53
International Falls, MN 56649
(218) 283 6600
Rainy Lake Visitor Center
(218) 286 5258
www.nps.gov/voya

WIND CAVE NATIONAL PARK
26611 US Highway 385
Hot Springs, SD 57747
(605) 745 4600
www.nps.gov/wica

WRANGELL-ST. ELIAS NATIONAL
PARK AND PRESERVE
P.O. Box 439
Copper Center, AK 99573
(907) 822 5234
www.nps.gov/wrst

YELLOWSTONE NATIONAL PARK
P.O. Box 168
Yellowstone National Park, WY 82190
(307) 344 7381
www.nps.gov/yell

YOSEMITE NATIONAL PARK
P.O. Box 577
Yosemite National Park, CA 95389
(209) 372 0200
www.nps.gov/yose

ZION NATIONAL PARK
Springdale, UT 84767
(435) 772 3256
Backcountry information
(435) 772 0170
www.nps.gov/zion

INDEX

ACKNOWLEDGMENTS

Quercus Editions Ltd
Carmelite House
50 Victoria Embankment
London
EC4Y 0DZ

First published in 2009
Copyright © Quercus Publishing 2009
Text by Mel White

A catalogue record of this book is available from the
British Library.

ISBN: 978-1-78648-251-8

Manufactured in China

10 9 8 7 6 5 4 3 2

Created for Quercus by Tall Tree Ltd
Art director: Ed Simkins
Additional cartography: David Broad and Nick Rowland
Indexer: Dorothy Frame

PICTURE CREDITS

GI = Getty Images
t = top, b = bottom, c = center, l = left, r = right

4–5 Alex Soh Photography/GI; 8 Jeff Foott/GI; 10–11 and
11t Darrell Gulin/GI; 11b Cosmo Condina/GI; 12–13 Adam
Jones/GI; 14–15 Jeff Foott/GI; 15t and 15b Jake Wyman/
GI; 16 Beth Davidow/GI; 16–17 Melissa Farlow/GI; 18–19
Philippe Bourseiller/GI; 20 Comstock/GI; 21t Altrendo
Nature/GI; 21b Raymond Gehman/GI; 22–23 Panoramic
Images/GI; 24l Norbert Rosing/GI; 24–25 George F.
Mobley/GI; 25 Jeff Foott/GI; 26–27 Nancy Nehring/GI; 27
Stephen Alvarez/GI; 28–29 Altrendo Travel/GI; 29 Adam
Jones/GI; 30–31 JupiterImages/GI; 32–33 Raul Touzon/GI;
32 Stan Osolinski/GI; 33 Renaud Visage/GI; 34–35 Jeff
Hunter/GI; 34 Brandon Cole/GI; 35 George Grall/GI; 36–37
Randy Wells/GI; 37t Rosemary Calvert/GI; 37b Eddie
Brady/GI; 38–39 Panoramic Images/GI; 39 Jeff Hunter/GI;
40–41 and 41t Buddy Mays/CORBIS, 41b Jeff Greenberg/
Alamy; 42 Philip Schermeister/GI; 43 Eddie Soloway/GI;
44–45 Richard Olsenius/GI; 45 Joseph Van Os/GI; 46–47
Panoramic Images/GI; 48–49 Willard Clay/GI; 49t Jake
Rajs/GI; 49b Michael Melford/GI; 50–51 Sergio Pitamitz/GI;
51 G. Richard Kettlewell/GI; 52–53t, 52, 53t and 53b
National Park Service Photo; 52–53b Panoramic Images/
GI; 54–55 Adam Jones/GI; 56–57 Panoramic Images/GI;
56 Skip Brown/GI; 57 James Hager/GI; 58–59 Michele
Falzone/GI; 60–61 Jeff Foott/GI; 61t Julian Pottage/GI;
61b Norbert Rosing/GI; 62–63 Cornelia Doerr/GI; 64–65
Michele Falzone/GI; 65t Anna Henly/GI; 65b Art Wolfe/GI;
66–67 Josiah Davidson/GI; 68 Mark Lewis/GI; 69t
Stockbyte/GI; 69b Ruth Tomlinson/GI; 70–71 Macduff
Everton/GI; 71t Paul McCormick/GI; 72t Grant Faint/GI;
72–73 Randall Levensaler/GI; 74–75 Philippe Bourseiller/
GI; 76–77 Lewis Kemper/GI; 77t Comstock/GI; 77b Paul
Nicklen/GI; 78–79 Adam Jones/GI; 80–81 Jack Dykinga/
GI; 81t Walter Meayers Edwards/GI; 81b Michael Nichols/
GI; 82 Jeremy Woodhouse/GI; 82–83 Witold Skrypczak/GI;
84–85 and 86–87 Ian Shive/GI; 87t Charles Melton/GI;
87b Kerrick James Photog/GI; 88–89 Cosmo Condina/GI;
90t Pete Ryan/GI; 91t James Hager/GI; 90bl, 90br, 91bl
and 91br National Park Service Photo; 92–93 Raimund
Linke/GI; 93 Tim Laman/GI; 94–95 David Muench/GI; 94

Panoramic Images/GI; 95l and 95c National Park Service
Photo; 95r Purestock/GI; 96–97 De Agostini/GI; 98–99
James Randklev/GI; 98 Joe McDonald/GI; 99 Paul Damien/
GI; 100–101 James Randklev/GI; 102 Panoramic Images/
GI; 103t Joseph Van Os/GI; 103b Time & Life Pictures/GI;
104–105 Bill Hatcher/GI; 105 Harald Sund/GI; 106–107
Roine Magnusson/GI; 108 Ralph Lee Hopkins/GI; 109t Roy
Toft/GI; 109b National Park Service Photo; 110–111 and
112–113 Ralph Lee Hopkins/GI; 112 Altrendo Nature/GI;
113l National Park Service Photo; 113r Frank Greenaway/
GI; 114–115 Stephen Studd/GI; 116–117 David Muench/GI;
117t Tim Flach/GI; 117b Joe & Mary Ann McDonald/GI;
118–119 Jeff Hunter/GI; 120 Enrique Aguirre/GI; 121t Jeff
Foott/GI; 121b and 122–123 Rich Reid/GI; 122 David
Courtenay/GI; 123 James A. Sugar/GI; 124–125 DEA/M.
SANTINI/GI; 126–127 Phil Schermeister/GI; 127t Joanna
McCarthy/GI; 127b Jeff Foott/GI; 128–129 Darrell Gulin/GI;
130t Paul Souders/GI; 130b Rich Reid/GI; 131 Altrendo
Panoramic/GI; 132–133 Michele Falzone/GI; 134–135
Mary Liz Austin/GI; 136–137 Paul Nicklen/GI; 137t Walter
Bibikow/GI; 137b Don Smith/GI; 138–139 Timothy
Hearsum/GI; 138 Altrendo Travel/GI; 140–141 Joseph
McNally/GI; 141 M. DeFreitas/GI; 142–143 Altrendo
Panoramic/GI; 142 Peter Chadwick/GI; 144–145 Alan
Kearney/GI; 146–147 Philippe Bourseiller/GI; 146 Andy
Rouse/GI; 147 Neal Mishler/GI; 148–149 Alan
Majchrowicz/GI; 150–151 Panoramic Images/GI; 150
Purestock/GI; 151 James Hager/GI; 152–153 Ethan Welty/
GI; 154–155 JH Pete Carmichael/GI; 155t Georgette
Douwma/GI; 155b Panoramic Images/GI; 156–157 Ethan
Welty/GI; 157 Darrell Gulin/GI; 158–159 Macduff Everton/
GI; 160–161 Paul Souders/GI; 161t Johnny Johnson/GI;
161b Riccardo Savi/GI; 162–163 Art Wolfe/GI; 164–165t
National Geographic/GI; 164–165b Michael S. Quinton/GI;
165 Walter Bibikow/GI; 166–167 Michael Melford/GI; 166
Paul Souders/GI; 168–169 Kevin Schafer/GI; 169 Harald
Sund/GI; 170–171 Purestock/GI; 171 Michael DeYoung/GI;
172–173 Bryce Pincham/GI; 174 Johnny Johnson/GI; 175t
Joseph Van Os/GI; 175b Gary Vestal/GI; 176 AFP/GI; 177
Eric Rorer/GI; 178–179 Michael Melford/GI; 179 Tom
Walker/GI; 180–181 Stephen Alvarez/GI; 182 Altrendo
Nature/GI; 183t Art Wolfe/GI; 183b Chris Johns/GI;
184–185 Mary Liz Austin/GI; 185 James Randklev/GI;
186–187 Randy Olson/GI; 187 Paul Chesley/GI.